Internet Solutions for Project Managers

Wiley Operations Management Series for Professionals

Other published titles in this series are:

Internet Solutions for Project Managers

Amit K. Maitra

John Wiley & Sons, Inc.

New York • Chichester • Weinheim • Brisbane • Singapore • Toronto

This book is printed on acid-free paper. ∞

Copyright © 2000 by Amit K. Maitra. All rights reserved.

Published by John Wiley & Sons, Inc.

Published simultaneously in Canada.

This publication is designed to provide accurate and authoritative information in regard to the subject matter covered. It is sold with the understanding that the publisher is not engaged in rendering legal, accounting, or other professional services. If legal advice or other expert assistance is required, the services of a competent professional person should be sought.

Library of Congress Cataloging-in-Publication Data

Maitra, Amit K., 1947-
Internet solutions for project managers/Amit K. Maitra.
   p.   cm.—(Wiley operations management series for professionals)
   Includes bibliographical references and index.
   ISBN 0-471-33027-2 (cloth : alk. paper)
   1. Industrial project management—Computer network resources. 2. Internet (Computer network) 3. Internet service providers. 4. Web servers. I. Title. II. Series.
HD69.P75M35   1999
004.67'8—dc21   99-29529

Printed in the United States of America.

10 9 8 7 6 5 4 3 2 1

In memory of my uncle,
Dr. Karuna K. Maitra, who
encouraged me to reach for the stars,
while keeping my feet on the ground.

Contents

Preface

A fundamental change is taking place in the nature and application of the Internet in business. This change has profound and far-reaching implications for your organization and for you, the project manager. As a facilitator of communications, the Internet is indispensable for improving productivity and profitability in today's business environment.

There is much more to the art of using the Internet than just a mere e-mail application or home page on a web site to gain a competitive advantage for advertising purposes. The Internet, driven by demands of the new competitive business environment, is forcing enterprises to integrate data, text, voice, and image information in various formats, and also to be open and networked. It is dynamic, based on interchangeable parts, and it technologically empowers users by distributing decision making in all functions, including project management. The Internet provides a backbone for team-oriented business structures. A shift is occurring in the nature of enterprises and how they gather, maintain, use, and update their data and information.

The motivation for this book is to make project and operations managers who want to view the current status of all active projects at a single glance aware of Internet capabilities. Whether their team is located in the same building or across the globe, the Internet can facilitate project management to:

- Scope out all tasks for a project in advance.
- Track a project's progress and adjust the timeline in real time as schedules change.

- Understand resource bottlenecks and adjust the plan accordingly.
- Work from anywhere or on any platform.

Internet Solutions for Project Managers describes the types of approaches and applications that the Internet makes available to project and operations managers in all types of businesses—both "brick-and-mortar" and Internet. Second, it addresses the technical and management issues that must be tackled to ensure effective and profitable project development. This book covers many topics of interest: (a) the application of the Internet for managing projects; (b) the importance of project management of an Internet Service Provider business, along with the technical and management issues that must be tackled to ensure its profitability and success.

The reader is provided insight on various issues, including: Project Home Pages that connect to a database of work in progress, field reports, spec sheets, financial reporting, and time sheets. These pages are usually secured from unauthorized persons; however, based on a "need-to-know" justification, customers, suppliers, vendors, and others may be allowed access to the appropriate Project Pages. This access allows inexpensive and immediate communication between distant team members to keep them constantly updated on project status, and enables both home-based and off-site project managers to monitor work in progress. Through case studies, the book explains the process that some enterprises are undertaking and presents guidelines to help others as they embark on a similar mission.

This book also discusses the infrastructure on which Internet project management applications designed specifically for persons away from their offices or for the Internet Service Providers (ISPs) could be built. Here, the focus is on mobile users, to make better use of the Internet medium to manage projects in their particular industry sectors (e.g., manufacturing, processing, utilities, etc.) and on Internet Service Providers, to manage their business in a more cost-effective way.

Various satellite technologies are finding newer implementations, depending on the Internet applications/services. We are witnessing the shift of the Internet from a static platform to a highly available platform with variable consistency and mobile databases. Current efforts focus on building persistent, collaborative applications that include shared calendars, documents, and other databases, and on collaborative program development to meet the project management needs of users in a mobile wireless computing environment. Through the ICO Global Communications (which is developing narrowband satellite system) case study, the book provides an assessment of the satellite data systems market, with strategic insight into the complex international telecommunications marketplace. In this book, ICO's proposed system will be profiled, the demand for international data services and mobile telephony forecasted, and the impact of ICO's system assessed. This book will emphasize the development of project management applications for the Internet that can make dramatic impacts in isolated rural areas in the developing countries of Asia, Africa, and Latin America.

Many ISPs are beginning to use off-the-shelf satellite data broadcast and caching technologies to deliver bandwidth-heavy applications, thereby avoiding bottlenecks imposed by the existing Internet infrastructure.

Several new satellite data delivery companies have emerged in recent months. Their service portfolios promise to free up bandwidth by both caching, which is a technique to reduce world-wide web network traffic and improve response time for end users, and updating the cache's contents through the satellite broadcast link. The book discusses caching, and through case studies of the service offerings of the new satellite data delivery companies such as SkyCache, it illustrates the potential of freeing up 30 to 60 percent of bandwidth, thereby forestalling the ISPs' need to purchase more leased lines. From the standpoint of managing and delivering a business solution, this last point holds the key to greater success. It indicates how caching will impact the business performance of ISPs, how their bottom line will be kept to a manageable monthly amount, and why they will not incur large capital costs for hardware and software, or hidden costs for support and updates.

Amit K. Maitra

Acknowledgments

Numerous individuals and organizations have contributed to this book, but only a few can be mentioned here.

I owe a great deal to Volunteers in Technical Assistance (VITA), InterAction, and ICO Global Communications for both inspiration and information. Gary L. Garriott, Director of Informatics, at VITA, has been an invaluable source of commentary and advice. He and Wayne Breslyn, MIS Director, InterAction, have been of great assistance through their work on Compendium of Information: InterAction Disaster Communications Workshop. This compendium has provided a valuable source of current data and insightful analysis on satellite Internet application, based on narrowband systems.

Pat McDougal, Senior Vice President of Strategic Business Development, ICO Global Communications, has been a continuing source of ideas. He and his associate Lisa Wagner increased my understanding of technology strategies as they commented perceptively on the ICO case development concerning its planned and proposed narrowband satellite system.

Countless other individuals provided invaluable help and support, both personally and professionally. I must single out Jeanne Glasser and Neil Levine, Senior Editors at John Wiley & Sons, who have been both catalysts of new ideas and peerless friends. Jeanne helped me sharpen my thinking and offered valued support for this book. Her assistant, Debra Alpern, made my relationship with John Wiley a delightful one. Matt Belovarich, my colleague and manager at Atlantic Science and Technology Corporation, and Jeff Smallwood and William Thrift (also from

Atlantic Science and Technology Corporation) helped me with the illustrations in various chapters. Larry Meyer and Laura Ho of Hermitage Publishing Services and their editors did a thorough job in a remarkably short period of time.

I have drawn on the work of a number of peers and colleagues, but there are several to whom I am particularly indebted. They are: Adedeji Bodunde Badiru, Richard Mathieu, "Doctor Bob" Rankin, Ross Tyner, Robert E. Lee, Mike Jensen, Mark Wood, Scott Clavena, Dr. Jerry Lucas, Doug Humphrey, Tom Wilson, Nathan J. Muller, Wendy D. White, Dr. Roger Rogard, Thomas Caldwell, Syed Ali, Preetham Peter, Jin White, Dr. Paul Strassmann, and Professors Barry G. Evans and Enrico Del Re.

Additionally, as I continue to work with industry developers and marketers, I owe special thanks to them for their openness and their contributions. When I needed, they were there to provide support by releasing illustrative materials, including charts, diagrams, and viewgraphs for use in this new book. Colleen Kelly at Primavera Systems, Barbara Tallent at Netmosphere, Nathan Trueblood at Energy Interactive, David Dietrich at Electric Power Research Institute (EPRI) Journal, David Bowermaster and Roger Nyhus at Teledesic, Reid Stephenson and Bob Weideman at Globalstar, and Lloyd Wood at Lloyd's Satellite Constellations, United Kingdom, have been particularly helpful in assisting me with the completion of this book. I do appreciate their help and guidance.

The most important acknowledgment comes last. My wife, Julie Binder Maitra, has aided me beyond measure. Without her support, I would still be staring at a blank piece of paper. She is my most demanding critic as well as my main inducement for focusing on the key points of the entire manuscript. As I continually bring new deadlines into an already busy home environment, she has to be admired and recognized for her patience and continued assistance.

Without all of you, writing this book would have been impossible. Thanks to you all!

Introduction

The Scope of this Book

More than 300 books are now available that contain the word "Internet," or related terms such as "Intranet," "Extranet," or the world wide web in their titles. The challenge for enterprises that want to (1) make use of the Internet as a project management tool, or (2) serve the Internet end users is to find a book that describes the application of Internet-based project management, including the current modes of mobile access for special circumstances via Internet-over-Satellite services, and caching system that saves the Internet Service Provider a lot of money for their expensive, high speed Internet connections. Relax, your search is over.

In today's global marketplace, fundamental changes aimed at improved performance are essential for survival. *Internet Solutions for Project Managers* offers up-to-date, practical approaches for significantly improving the operational performance of an enterprise in which

1. Team members interact, have access to desired information at appropriate times, and maintain a shared vision about their project while remaining focused on individual tasks.
2. Team members can express and measure individual and group progress in meeting project objectives.
3. New team members "get up to speed" on the project history without disrupting other team members.
4. Team members can draw on the experience of similar projects when making project-related decisions.

The case studies, which form a major strength of the book, include:

1. Manufacturing and the Internet cases that demonstrate how manufacturing organizations are using the Internet for project planning, communication, coordination, and control. Ample graphical representations are used to illustrate how executives see a high-level overview of all projects on the Internet, how the status of projects can be easily updated by either importing Action Plan project data or by entering the information into a dialog box, and how team members can access all project-related information.

2. ICO Global Communications' plan and proposal for a Medium Earth Orbiting (MEO) satellite system for the rapidly growing market for mobile telephony. MEO satellites, with concomitant low-cost hardware, can make a dramatic impact in isolated rural areas. Such areas are currently excluded from the "Internet revolution," because most isolated regions outside North America and western Europe have no connectivity of any kind, including e-mail. Major satellite vendors, including Motorola, Lockheed Martin, Hughes, Alcatel Espace, and Loral have proposed a number of broadband satellite systems. Their emphasis is on bandwidth capacities to accommodate world wide web applications, which are available to most developed countries. What is being overlooked in this scenario is the usefulness and availability of e-mail-based access to Internet information protocols such as file transfer (FTP), search engines, and the web itself. This includes the provision of such services through communications satellites in medium-earth orbit, with corresponding low-cost hardware for mobile users in developing regions of the world. Herein lies the purpose, usefulness, and timeliness of the ICO case study.

3. The service offerings of the new satellite data delivery companies such as SkyCache. This case material illustrates the potential of freeing up 30 to 60 percent of bandwidth, thereby forestalling the ISPs' need to purchase more leased lines. From the standpoint of managing and delivering a business solution, this last point holds the key to greater success because it demonstrates

how caching will impact the business performance of ISPs, how their bottom line will be kept to a manageable amount per month, and why they will not incur large capital costs for hardware and software, or hidden costs for support and updates.

Internet Solutions for Project Managers is a book with an important difference. In this, the author demonstrates the incorporation of: (1) Internet-based project management techniques, including accessing the Internet by means of satellites; and (2) satellite-based caching service that promises to improve ISP's business by reducing bandwidth usage and lowering bandwidth costs, and fulfilling customers' needs with improved Internet performance. Complete with numerous illustrations, this book equips engineers, managers, and analysts in engineering, research and development, purchasing, distribution, operations, materials and planning units inside manufacturing or other types of enterprises, including the ISP organizations, with the tools they need to effectively manage all aspects of a project/business.

Each chapter contains useful information, including detailed case studies that provide insight into how different companies and ISPs are using the Internet to gather information, increase project/business success through visibility and analysis, manage a distributed team, and track project status and save bandwidth by identifying the most frequently requested web pages. You will learn how to:

- Link project milestones through project summaries
- E-mail task reminders
- Define roles
- Highlight complete and overdue tasks
- Filter views by resource, data range, overdue tasks
- Utilize e-mail-based access to Internet information protocols, if and when the situations demand, and employ some of the tools such as file transfer (FTP) and search engines, "hidden" by the ease of web access, for project management in remote and rural areas of the world.

The Internet and its special application—project management—can be the key to your company's success, but only if you know how to use it to your particular advantage. Above and beyond the critical factors identified previously, this book will provide an additional input. It will delineate how an ISP business will benefit from the caching phenomenon and from an improvement in end-user service performance and consequently higher market share.

Audience

The audiences for this book are operations managers, technology managers, project managers, and their supervisors. Secondary audiences are managers of business development, network planning, engineering, marketing and sales, product and systems development, who want to make informed judgments about the Internet, including its special application in project management. These business, project, and technical managers will guide enterprises in developing, specifying, and aligning the plethora of Internet information tools into a single virtually unified hosting platform customized to the specific project management needs of their enterprise. These managers will, therefore, benefit from a better understanding of the competitive advantages of satellite Internet delivery in situations where existing delivery is no longer practical or economical. This book addresses the impact of latency for Internet delivery and provides the latest intelligence on the hottest satellite data delivery projects and their applications for Internet delivery.

The Organization of This Book

This book departs from the usual presentation style of other available Internet books, which describe the various solutions and then propose some techniques to get your business moving in that direction. This book is meant to be a starting place for further investigation and should be viewed as a useful resource in terms of:

- What project management functions are best addressed by the Internet?

- How should one use the Internet tools, such as e-mail, File Transfer Protocol (FTP), and the world wide web (WWW), for project management purposes?

- Why should one use the Internet: Better Return on Investment/Return on Management?

- When should one assess satellite transmission for Internet provisions?

- Where are the good results: case histories of real-life experiences of the Internet as a project management tool, hottest satellite projects and their applications for Internet delivery.

In order for a business to do well with the Internet and its special application in project management, the technology must be clearly understood. Accordingly, Part I provides conceptual information and explains how each tool works and how the tool is used in the Internet community with appropriate addition of embedded or external security features.

At this stage of Internet medium evolution, it is unnecessary to refer to its early history—that is, how the network was initially conceived and used in the defense research environment. The Internet Society web site is an excellent place to review that type of information.

On another related subject, this book is intended for those who wish to explore how organizations are using or could use the Internet to create strategic opportunities for project management. It is not directed at systems engineers or programmers who are creating Enterprise Internet by designing and implementing Transmission Control Protocol/Internet Protocol (TCP/IP) routing architectures and infrastructures and attendant security features. Although these technical details are essential in setting and implementing effective Internet services, Chapter 1 deliberately leaves treatment of those issues to other sources. It provides some pointers in that direction, with references to appropriate web sites.

Chapter 2 explores the two themes of Internet provision via satellite: project management applications based on Internet provisions via satellite and the technical challenges of caching and the latest applications of caching for managing Internet Service Provider (ISP) businesses.

Part II includes case studies of the project management applications available through the Internet medium.

Because the Internet is now a robust medium, an organization must develop new strategies to utilize it. "New strategies" mean different things to different people. For instance, IBM announced an Enterprise Internet Initiative that would enable large, medium, and small companies to integrate the Internet into their computing infrastructures. Back in 1995, this initiative was a comprehensive service option available to a company to implement Internet components that enabled "standard" interfaces to e-mail, FTP, Telnet, Mosaic with the world wide web (WWW), USENET Newsgroups, and also to Internet Relay Chat (IRC). Similarly, most other references to enterprise-wide Internet strategy development focus on the specific technology aspect of the Internet such as Navigating the Net, SLIP/PPP connection, and such.

Although technology focus is crucial, the Internet is now open to individuals and businesses in marketing, customer service, human resources, security and legal, as well as the technical experts within the Information Services division of an enterprise, provided they abide by Acceptable Use Policies (AUP) delineated in Appendix A. The case studies document how the organizations and the players in them target the best business applications of the Internet medium. Chapters 3, 4, and 5 provide three case studies. The first one relates to project management in a manufacturing environment, and the other two assess the latest applications for Internet provision via satellite.

Part III sets the guidelines for opportunity identification that will result in improved Return on Investments (ROI). It addresses ROI by looking at the cost of time and information, and then formulating a mechanism to capture all the hard-to-measure items such as time saved, customer service, and management productivity improvements that caching or the satellite-based data deliver for ISP businesses.

The extraordinary changes in the cost of processing, storing, and distributing information are transforming every aspect of the ISP business environment. This is an excellent time to learn about a whole new way of doing business. The challenge is to determine some of the benefits that could be realized from switching to caching and satellite-based data delivery.

Chapter 6 documents how the ulilities are extending their customer service and/or marketing-related project management activities over the Internet.

Chapter 7 explains how management productivity improves through caching and its associated application, the satellite-based data delivery, and recommends a new measure—Return On Management (ROM).

The appendixes provide more technical definitions, information on hardware, software issues, security concerns and requirements, and discuss specific managerial issues.

PART I

THE INTERNET

.

CHAPTER 1
Making the Internet Work

The Internet is changing the way people in private, public, and international organizations conduct business. Global access to people, data, software, documents, graphics, audio, and video clips allow organizations to communicate with experts throughout the world, and to receive immediate support for any technical problems. Since the publication of *Developing a Corporate Internet Strategy: The IT Manager's Guide* in 1996,[1] the Internet has been growing by leaps and bounds. The Internet has been instrumental in ushering the era of direct person-to-person communication through electronic mail (e-mail) and group communication with electronic communication forums (user groups). Additionally, many computers on the Internet store information that is freely accessible, thereby facilitating and accelerating the process of sharing, disseminating, and acquiring information. It is beyond the scope of this chapter to provide detailed coverage of all the recent extensions in the Internet's capabilities. The reader should not think that all the recent developments have been discussed in full. Rather, this chapter investigates the Internet's major elements, as they are available today, at a depth sufficient to permit a sound appraisal.*

Accessing the Internet

In order for one to use the Internet, one must first access it. Today, most organizations in the industrialized countries of the world provide Inter-

* In this effort the author is particularly indebted to Richard G. Mathieu and Adedeji Bodunde Badin.

net access to their employees. These organizations and their employees may use specialized Internet access firms, called Internet Service Providers (ISPs), and commercial online services, such as CompuServe, America Online, and the Microsoft Network. The commercial online services are increasingly integrating their own content with that of the Internet; they want to be more successful, and integration influences their decision to achieve that goal.

Access to the Internet can be provided by any local, regional, or national ISP, at whatever rates they set. Some services are expensive, so the different organizations must identify the features that are important to them. To that end, Table 1.1 identifies the various types of Internet Service Providers and their characteristics.

Types of Internet Access

In general, there are three levels of service: e-mail only, dial-up access, and direct permanent attachment. Technically, there are multiple options available for securing these service levels. This section describes the six commonly exercised options. Appendix B provides more details on the hardware and software issues.

REMOTE NETWORK ACCESS OR GATEWAY OR ONLINE SERVICES

America Online, Delphi, CompuServe, Genie, MCI Mail, and some commercial Bulletin Board Services (BBS), such as FidoNet, are examples of Gateway Services. They provide limited Internet access. This type of access is not suitable for business users, because most commercial providers, as well as the BBS, are simply gateways to Internet e-mail. They are not *on* the Internet, and consequently there are significant delays in mail delivery, size limitations on e-mail messages, and limitations on real Internet access. This last problem may be corrected in the near future.

DIAL-UP OR SHELL ACCOUNTS

This is the simplest and least expensive way of accessing the Internet. Equipment needs are very modest for this type of connectivity. This

Table 1.1 The Five Types of Internet Service Providers

Type of Internet Service Provider	Examples	Characteristics
Interexchange Carriers (IXCs), Value-added Networks	Sprint, MCI Communications, Advantis, AT&T	Ubiquitous service, full-time help desks. Provider manages and maintains network, including hardware and leased lines. Highest level of quality customer support.
Large Commercial Internet Providers (CIPs)	Advanced Network & Services, Inc. (ANS); Performance Systems International, Inc. (PSI); UUNet Technologies, Inc. (Alternet).	Coverage is throughout United States. Access is through leased lines from 56 Kbps to 1.544 Mbps, frame relay, ISDN, coaxial cable in selected location, async dial-up. Provider will manage equipment, configure domain name server, e-mail gateway, FTP server, furnish space on its own FTP servers, and provide consulting services.
Regional Providers	The Pipeline, Merit Network, Inc., PREPNet, Real-Time Communications, Texas MetroNet, Teleport SSNet Inc.	Often spin-offs of academic providers, generally inexperienced staff, uncertain customer support.
Online Services	America Online (AOL), Delphi, Prodigy, CompuServe, Genie, ImagiNation, ZiffNet	Offer a variety of features and services, such as news, weather, sports, shopping, travel arrangements, bulletin boards (also called forums or roundtables) on many interests, games, online chatting, investment advice and services, educational services, reference works and more. Some of these deliver integrated Internet business solutions.
Bulletin Board Systems	35,000+ in North America	Typically local dial-in, may have "door" to the Internet.

Source: Amit K. Maitra, *Building A Corporate Internet Strategy: The IT Manager's Guide,* John Wiley & Sons, December 1997.

option meets most of the needs of small to medium-sized enterprises that are not computer intensive, and it is equally suitable for some functions of larger businesses.

This type of connection is often referred to as indirect, because the dial-up connection is handled through another computer that is a part of the Internet. The process begins with a user dialing a phone number for a "remote" computer (meaning that it is other than the user's own computer, not that it is far away; it could be in the same room as the user's computer, but it would still be considered remote). After answering several questions, the user is connected to the computer's Internet connection to obtain the desired information. Users are typically billed on a per-hour basis, although some Internet providers offer flat-rate service. The advantages are low cost for users and minimal hardware and software requirements. A drawback is that some services that use graphical interfaces aren't available to dial-up sessions.

SERIAL LINE INTERNET PROTOCOL (SLIP)

This is a dial-up direct connection service that uses normal phone lines, modems, and special software packages conforming to SLIP standards. This mode of connection is superior to dial-up because: (1) SLIP can be attached to an enterprise's local area network (LAN), allowing for multiple users; (2) the users' system is actually connected to the Internet as a node, so users can avail themselves of all Internet services; (3) users need not concern themselves with the details and protocols of working with a remote host; and (4) access tools run on the user's system rather than on a remote host.

The telephone charges are modest, requiring only a normal phone line. The up-front equipment costs are somewhat higher than for simple dial-up, requiring a 486 PC or a Macintosh Quadra. In this particular setup, the service provider is acting only as an intermediate connection point, so users must have a computer with independent storage and sufficient performance to host necessary software, and a high-speed modem—9,600 baud minimum, 14,400 or 28,800 recommended. Users are generally billed on a per-hour basis, although some Internet providers offer flat-rate service.

POINT TO POINT PROTOCOL (PPP)

This is the functional replacement for SLIP. The Internet standard Point to Point Protocol (PPP) corrects many of the deficiencies in SLIP. For instance, PPP is faster and more stable, prompting many network providers to offer PPP as the sole access protocol for a cost-effective mechanism for corporate Internet connections.

INTEGRATED SERVICES DIGITAL NETWORK (ISDN)

This is an increasingly popular means of connecting to the Internet. ISDN represents a completely digital connection all the way from the phone company to the customer premises, resulting in a more reliable connection at much higher speeds. A basic rate ISDN line provides a digital connection consisting of two 64 kilobytes per second (Kbps) B channels. ISDN's multichannel lines allow the user to make more than one connection at a time. For example, one can talk on the phone with one of the B channels, while simultaneously using the Internet on the other. Conversely, both channels can be bonded to obtain a single 128 Kbps signal.

ISDN does not circumvent the ISPs. Rather, to install ISDN, the cooperation of both the local telephone company and the ISP is needed. The phone company must first install an ISDN line on the customer's premises. It will then install a network terminal device to convert the ISDN signal into something that the computer can use. To make the connection from the computer to the network terminal device, a terminal adapter is needed, which is the digital equivalent of a modem. Many newer terminal adapters now have a built-in network terminal device. An ISDN line is more expensive than a traditional analog phone line, but for frequent Internet users the advantages outweigh the costs.

Other options for direct connections include Frame Relay, Asynchronous Transfer Mode (ATM), satellite links, microwave links, and CATV links. Satellite links offer particular advantages for less developed countries of the world and warrant special treatment of the subject. Following a summary description of dedicated lines that allow direct permanent attachment to the Internet, a separate and exclusive section will discuss the topic in greater details.

DEDICATED LEASED LINES AND REGISTERING AS AN INTERNET NODE

This level of connection is designed to service a large number of users with a heavy amount of traffic. Dedicated leased lines are recommended for large enterprises or corporations because they offer complete access to all Internet facilities as a node, with virtually no limit to the number of users. This type of connection is suitable for enterprises that need to move large amounts of data, that want to publish data on the Internet, or have very demanding performance requirements.

These lines are frequently referred to as 56KB, T-1, or T-3. The costs for setting up and running a high-speed dedicated line are much higher; but they are the most powerful and flexible Internet connections. Table 1.2 provides a brief summary of the different types of Internet connections.

Many businesses wish to use their company names as a node name, such as Satlink.com. There are two ways to become a true node: (1) through a full dedicated line connection and (2) through certain full-time SLIP connections. However, many dial-up service providers allow companies to have domain names through the use of an alias, which allows a company to appear as though it is Satlink.com without actually being a node.

Domain names are Internet "addresses" that are assigned on a first-come, first-served basis. To start a new Internet node, an enterprise must first contact Inter-networking Information Center (InterNIC) of Network Solutions, Inc. of Herndon, Virginia, for a domain name, as well as for fees and other pertinent information. InterNIC assigns and keeps

Table 1.2 Internet Connections and Phone Line Types

Connection	Speed	Features
Gateways Dial-up	0-28.8 Kbps	May temporarily be placed on the Internet.
SLIP PPP	0-28.8 Kbps	Employs local software on the user's own computer, allowing for Graphical User Interfaces that make the Internet easier to use for novices.
ISDN	Up to 128 Kbps	Provides reliable digital service. Guarantees 64 or 128 Kbps transport speed to the ISP for uninterrupted Internet connection.
Leased line	56 Kbps to 768 Kbps	Provides most direct connection to the Internet—server is actually on the Internet.

track of all domain names in the United States. Under contract with the National Science Foundation since April 1993, it administers a registration process that includes the creation of a database which maps the names to the numbers used for Internet routing. Because of the ever increasing number of applicants, there are several weeks' delay in the processing time. Once the domain name is registered, the enterprise is able to use it.

Satellite Internet Access

In view of the phenomenal growth of the Internet, some access providers are seriously considering satellite technology as an option to offer customers faster access to the Internet web pages. Assuming the current trend continues, in a few years most of the material one accesses via the Internet could be transmitted by satellite.

Satellites offer several advantages over landlines in transmitting and receiving large amounts of data. The primary advantage is speed: Because there is no physical link between the satellite and a receiving station on the ground, there is no inherent physical limit as to how much bandwidth can be supplied to each customer.

The only limit to transmission bandwidth is the data capability of the satellite itself. If a customer needs more bandwidth, it is possible to provide that with almost no waiting period. A T3 (45M-bps) connection is as quickly and easily installed as a 64K-bps connection; there is no need to wait for the phone company to install a line.

Coverage area is the second big advantage of satellites, which is why people living in remote areas have come to rely on them. A connection can be established anywhere within the satellite's broadcast footprint, provided the dish on the ground is pointed at the right part of the sky. The computer user connects his or her PC to a device similar to a conventional TV signal receiver, which in turn is connected to a dish on a roof, balcony, or a yard. When the user makes an "upstream" request for a web page or sends an outgoing message, it may still go to the ISP via a conventional phone line; however, the rest is all unidirectional "downstream" download. The incoming e-mail, newsgroup postings, software updates, and audio/video data are relayed to the user via a satellite—at speeds that make an ISDN (integrated services digital network) line look slow.

"Interactivity" may not be the most accurate term to describe the Internet environment. What is actually taking place is a form of customized "broadcast"—and broadcasting is a task that satellites are ideally suited for. PanAmSat, a pioneer in the broadcast satellite business, has become totally immersed in this new business, and it has become an integral part of the Internet in some areas of the world. The company now offers Internet services to ISPs and corporations, with impressive results. In 1998, Internet-related business accounted for about 10 percent of Êcorporate's income. PanAmSat's John Chesen predicts that, in the near future, as much as 40 percent of revenues could come from Internet and other data transmission services.

Another company currently offering a home-user satellite Internet reception system is DirectPC. The company's customers in North America are receiving Internet access at data transmission speeds of 400 Kbps. Customers use a parabolic antenna system, which they usually install themselves, and pay a monthly fee.

This service has a promising future because the multimedia features, including audio, video, and music, are becoming more and more common in web pages. For people who use multimedia and whose proportion of data received tends to exceed the data sent, satellite is the appropriate Internet access service.

Selecting the ISP

ISPs do not provide their own content to the subscribers. Instead, they offer high-speed access and flexible software options over a wide range of pricing options, including support for obtaining a direct leased line for an organization. Finding a good ISP requires comparative shopping, using the following criteria:

Criteria	Questions to Address
Ease of Installation	1. What software is needed to dial in to the provider?
	2. Is the interface easy?

3. How good is the technical support during installation?

4. Will the ISP arrange for telephone company installation and coordinate the installation of its services with the local telephone company for customers ordering leased lines?

Pricing

5. How much does the installation cost?

6. Does the ISP have a local access number?

7. Does it have multiple local access numbers in many key cities?

8. Does it offer toll-free access numbers for people traveling on business to different cities around the country?

9. Does the ISP charge a monthly flat fee or charge according to a graduated scale, based on the customer's usage?

10. How much additional money does the ISP charge for an ISDN service?

11. Does it offer any special deal on regular and/or ISDN service to new users?

12. Does the ISP have a warranty on the service for leased lines?

13. Does it guarantee a specific level of aggregate bandwidth all the way to the Internet?

Connection Speed

14. Does the ISP support 28.8 Kbps dial-up access?

15. Does it offer ISDN connection?

16. How reliable is the provider's connection?

17. Are the provider's dial-in lines always busy during peak hours?

Internet Tools

18. What does the ISP offer?
- Full world wide web (WWW) access
- File Transfer Protocol (FTP)
- Usenet news

- Telnet
- Web-page construction and/or hosting

19. Does the ISP impose any constraint on what web browser one can use: Netscape or Internet Explorer?

Technical Support 20. What kind of technical support does the provider offer?

- What happens when one calls for help?
- If there is no immediate answer, does someone from an upper-level technical support return a call within a few hours?

Content 21. While considering a commercial online service, the all-important question is:

- Does that service provide content specific to one's needs?

Getting Ready: Hardware, Operating Systems, and Internet Access Software

It is not the intent of this book to provide all technical details on this very important topic. Information systems professionals, who are specialists that address network architecture development issues, are better suited to identify the specific hardware, operating systems, and Internet access software requirements in a given environment. The author urges readers to consult the IS professionals in their respective organizations. The focus in the next few paragraphs is to identify basic requirements for the Internet connectivity.

Stated simply, for adequate performance, one needs:

- A PC—a 486/50 megahertz or faster CPU with at least 8 megabytes of RAM.
- A modem—minimum speed of 14.4 (14,400 bps). A faster modem with 28.8 (28,800 bps), however, significantly enhances the web browsing and downloading capabilities.

- A Windows-accelerated video card and a minimum 500 megabyte hard drive.
- Multimedia capability. This greatly enhances the web experience.
- A sound card with speakers, if audio experience is important.
- A 17-inch monitor. This size reduces eyestrain.
- Operating System for the PC (e.g., Windows 95/98, Windows NT, OS/2 Warp, etc.).
- Internet access tools. There are three choices:
  1. A suite of distinct modules
  2. An integrated package with a single interface
  3. A mix-and-match bundle one creates oneself

Configuring the software to make the connection to the Internet is usually the most difficult part of getting online. For example, if one is making a direct connection to the Internet, the person must know his/her IP address, Domain Name Server, and the address of his/her gateway and host. This information is provided by the ISP, but a nontechnical person should solicit the support of an organization's internal IS technical support personnel so that the information is inserted in the right order in the right window.

In addition to the items listed above, a user must also have the following:

- A world wide web browser (e.g., Netscape Navigator, Microsoft Internet Explorer)
- An e-mail program
- A Usenet newsreader
- An FTP client to download files
- A Telnet client for remote logins

It is possible to have e-mail only access to the Internet, but world wide web access is desirable in order to get the most out of the Internet. Windows 95/98 has made Internet access very easy by providing the necessary software to connect and transmit e-mail. The Microsoft Network bundled with Windows 95/98 gives access to newsgroups. Like Windows 95/98, OS/2 Warp makes it simple to connect to the Internet, but the wide selection of Internet software available for Windows is not available for OS/2.

The key to Internet access with the Macintosh is a fast modem and the right software. There is plenty to choose from: Zterm (telecom software), MacTCP (for TCP/IP compatibility), InterSLIP (for SLIP connectivity), Fetch (FTP program), TurboGopher (gopher software), Eudora (for e-mail), Mosaic (web browser), and Stuffit Expander (to unpack files).

Connecting with People: Electronic Mail, ListServs, Mailing Lists

Electronic mail, commonly referred to as e-mail, is an exchange of information and computer programs without incorporating postage. E-mail is very fast and thus very attractive to electronic customers! Messages are exchanged in minutes as opposed to days or even months using regular mail. With the varied use of e-mail today, businesses are taking advantage of this technology to send information to potential clients and customers. Essentially, this involves connecting an enterprise's server to the Internet, which sends e-mail using the Simple Mail Transfer Program (SMTP).

The e-mail information content could be an ongoing, specialized discussion of some sort, a regular mailing, a text file, or even software. For example, telephone conferences, not uncommon in today's business environment, are slowly being replaced by e-mail messages that are read and posted at convenient times and places. This reduces the considerable investment of time and effort in scheduling, planning, and discussion. E-mail is seen as greatly facilitating group conferencing by enabling the members to participate at various times and from various locations. E-mail derives its power from mailing lists and the software that generates them. A mailing list provides two things:

1. A list of mail recipients. A mailing list is often centered around a specific topic such as commerce, science, academia, or entertainment.

2. Automatic distribution of mail items to the hundreds or even thousands of "subscribers" on such a list. Listserv or Majordomo software handles these mailings by automatically placing subscription requests into a database and generating periodic mailings. The frequency of such mailings could be monthly, weekly, daily, or even hourly. These softwares run on certain specific platforms only. The IS department for an enterprise is the right place to inquire about the platform issues.

For those enterprises that do not have IS departments but find the idea of putting mailing lists to work in their businesses appealing, a service provider can, under contract, set up and maintain the list or simply provide server space if these enterprises have the in-house resources to maintain the list themselves.

The convenience of mailing lists has produced many practical and economical business uses. E-mail and mailing lists provide an opportunity for different enterprises to keep their customers up-to-date and interested in their products and services, and to respond to customers' questions as quickly as possible. Mailing lists are very cost-effective because the customers seek out the enterprises without the enterprises having to look for them.

ELECTRONIC MAGAZINES OR "E-ZINES"

E-Zines are do-it-yourself publishing that require little more than an e-mail account. Some enterprises may not need an entire magazine to market their businesses online, but the format is interesting and useful.

GROUP DISCUSSIONS

Discussion lists are somewhat similar to mailing lists. The major difference is that mailing lists are sent to subscribers in one batch, whereas discussion lists forward messages one at a time. Discussion lists can be helpful to businesses. IBM, for example, gains a solid marketing advantage merely by maintaining a forum that serves the needs of OS/2 users. A subscription to the OS/2 Users Mailing List provides 10 to 40 messages daily, all about OS/2. Subscribers respond to the person making the original inquiry or send their response back to the entire group. IBM, in turn, simply derives marketing benefits from the e-mail traffic.

FREQUENTLY ASKED QUESTIONS (FAQ)

Because businesses are often asked the same questions repeatedly, a pre-arranged set of answers is available. When customers send individual questions via e-mail, an administrative assistant can respond immediately to a query by using the Q & A format. This promotes good customer relations, since customers regard the enterprise as highly responsive.

No discussion on e-mail is complete without referring to its equalizing effect within a corporation. E-mail has created an openness within corporate environments that until recently was nonexistent. If we concentrate strictly on the business aspect of this phenomenon, reference could be made to some significant developments.

Remark

Internet isn't the only system that uses e-mail. Almost any computer network will allow you to exchange messages within the network.

The most common business use of Internet connectivity involves internal and external communications. By using an e-mail package over the Internet, enterprises can establish contact with branches and work teams at many locations and can have high-speed access to vendors and customers. This is a virtual community in which people who may never meet or even communicate find themselves conversing about substantive matters.

Most people now prefer to communicate by e-mail rather than by phone or postal mail, because at all levels, from CEO to mailroom clerk, they feel freer to participate in discussions about the business. A person who sends a message by e-mail is more likely to receive a quick but a thoughtful reply.

At a time when the Internet offers various means of communicating, the most commonly requested/required Internet service still remains e-mail. A note of warning: e-mail is one of the more abused services on the Internet and is the subject of industry-wide scrutiny and improvement. Computer Emergency Response Team (CERT), a clearinghouse for Internet vulnerabilities at Carnegie Mellon University, advises that the main abuse of e-mail is to gain access to other services running on the same machine. There are state-of-the-art technical solutions for e-mail security problems, but that is not the subject of this book. For those interested in learning more about these solutions, CERT Advisories, such as cert-advisry-request@cert.org or majordomo@greatcircle.com, would be the place to begin.

Connecting with People: Usenet Newsgroups

Several forms of discussion groups on the Internet cover a broad range of issues, including technical topics, politics, and a variety of social issues. USENET is like a local bulletin board system, where users regulate their own public discussions. The quality, accuracy, and usefulness of the information that the newsgroups generate vary widely, but there are a few newsgroups that are invaluable to network security administrators. These include sci.crypt, comp.security, alt.privacy, and comp.virus. These names suggest that the newsgroups are built on a hierarchy. The first part of any name refers to the top-level hierarchy, such as "alt" (alternative), "biz" (business), "comp" (computer-related), "misc" (miscellaneous), and "rec" (recreational). Group names include one more qualifier to differentiate them from other subgroups under the same hierarchy. There are more than 20,000 newsgroups, including many that are not carried at all sites.

USENET services are the favorites of the users, but the various alt.fan and alt.sex newsgroups are indicative of the trivial nature of the Internet. The range of topics in such groups is somewhat broad for some people's tastes, but two points should be underscored:

1. The "offending" newsgroups are not representative of overall Internet traffic.

2. An organization can limit the scope of USENET newsgroups to which its employees have access (see Appendix A: Internet Policy for the Enterprise for more information on this point).

APPLICATIONS AND TOOLS FOR FINDING AND RETRIEVING INFORMATION: FTP AND TELNET

Although an astronomical number of things can be done on the Internet and its internal variant—intranet—the most well-known activities are as follows.

File Transfer Protocol (FTP)

The method used to transfer files from one computer destination to another across the Internet is identified by the initials FTP. After e-mail, FTP probably creates the most traffic on the Internet. A user can log into remote computers, search multiple directories, and retrieve and store files, provided he or she has a valid ID and password with which to log on. Thus, the user can access a wealth of databases, programs, images, and other software resources (spreadsheet files, word processing files, graphics, etc.). If an enterprise does not want users storing files on its system, it can change the permissions to read only, leaving the administrator with the sole ability to move files to the FTP directory.

Similarly, an organization can make its business available on the Internet. This entails setting up the organization's FTP server, and once the server is enabled, a portion of the organization's systems directory structure will be open to the public. An organization can set up the FTP server to allow only a few privileged users to access its data via the Internet. The more popular configuration, however, is to allow "anonymous" FTP, where anyone entering their e-mail address as a password can enter the system. Under anonymous FTP, users have restrictions. They are allowed access to part of the file system typically in public areas. This refers to the contents of a directory named /pub, for which users have access to only a few commands for retrieving files and maneuvering within subdirectories.

An enterprise should treat FTP as a potentially powerful account that should be confined to areas that cannot do damage to anything other than what is on the immediate server. This sort of limitation enhances enterprise network security. From a security standpoint, FTP is unique among the Internet services in that it requires permission for a remote host to open a local connection. In the event a user breaks out of the captive account, the intruder cannot do much damage because the enterprise server is dedicated to FTP and thus the intruder will be unable to access other machines within the enterprise network.

Telnet

Telnet is a Transmission Control Protocol/Internet Protocol (TCP/IP) which an operator uses to connect to a remote computer and run a program somewhere on the Internet as if he were sitting at a terminal linked directly to the remote computer. The web or HTTP protocol and the FTP protocol allow a user to request specific files from remote computers, but not to actually be logged on as a user of that computer. With Telnet, a user logs on as a regular user with whatever privileges he may have been granted to the specific applications and data on that computer.

To accomplish this, the user enters the Telnet command with the remote computer address onto the user's own computer, if the user is already connected to the Internet or on to an Internet intermediary such as Delphi. A Telnet command request looks like this (the computer name is made up): telnet the.libraryat.harvard.edu. Once the Telnet command is entered, the computer runs software that uses Telnet protocol to make the connection between computers.

Like FTP, one can use Telnet in two ways: either to connect to a computer where one already has an account or to log on to a computer where the person is a stranger. If you are wondering why anyone would want to use Telnet to gain access to a computer where the user is already known, the answer is that Telnet can be a major convenience and save the individual money, especially if the user happens to be in a distant place (e.g., Taiwan) with an account with a computer service in Chicago.

Telnet is best when it allows access to computers on which the person has no account. There are some limitations that should be explained. Let us review the example of the Telnet command request mentioned above: telnet the.libraryat.harvard.edu. The result of this request would be an invitation to log on with a user ID and a prompt for a password. If accepted, the person making the request would be logged on just the same as any other user who used this computer daily.

Warning

There is a major difference between being invited into a new computer through Telnet and entering (or cracking) someone else's private files through the use of an unauthorized user ID and password. (A cracker is a person who deliberately breaks into someone else's computer systems.) With Telnet, one is asked to share other people's information in the spirit of mutual discovery. But if someone is cracking into a strange computer, that person is breaking the law.

Telnet is most often used by program developers and users who have a need for specific applications or data located at a particular host computer. The type of programs for which a person receives permission to use can vary. Programs can provide basic information like weather forecasts, or complicated scientific data on the latest in neural research. Telnet provides several services, each of which provides different forms of information.

Hytelnet allows a person to locate Telnet resources around the Internet. There are two versions of Hytelnet:

- A stand-alone version that could be easily downloaded and used on one's own computer. This version provides a large amount of information about Telnet sites and a copy is available through anonymous FTP.
- An Internet service that is accessible through the Telnet. This version enables the user to choose the Telnet site that has the required resources; the user is then connected to that site automatically. To gain access to the Internet version of Hytelnet, a person needs to use the WWW or a Gopher location which is defined later in this section.

There is a note of caution about possible security breaches: Login information may be captured through Telnet. To date, few network-specific attacks have taken place through Telnet, so for safety, an enterprise should allow Telnet connections only from approved outside hosts and with tokens or plan for encryption. Below is a listing of searching and indexing tools:

Gopher. To make proper use of the Internet's millions of pieces of information one needs help. Unless a person uses special tools and services, the search for any particular information can turn into a search for the proverbial needle in the haystack. The good news is that services are available through the Internet that can help one search or organize all the billion bits of information out there in the system. Gopher, for example, is a basic menu-based system, linking files on different computers throughout the Internet. It provides access to text documents and graphics.

There are the *older* Internet search mechanisms which search indexes of databases for documents based on file titles, key words, or subject areas. Many servers still make good use of these tools:

Wide Area Information System (WAIS). This allows the user to narrow searches by selecting a variety of sources. "Relevance feedback" is the embedded process that discards common words, and ranks relevant documents according to the level or quality of the match, thereby improving the search.

Archie. This is used for files accessible via anonymous FTP. Indices of files located at sites across the globe are generated by Archie servers. The users then receive an appropriate Archie site name, IP address, and the location within the archive to retrieve the desired file.

Veronica. This searches available Gopher sites for information on a specific topic.

WHOIS. This was originally founded by the Defense Data Network's Network Information Center. Now it is run by InterNIC Registration Services in Herndon, Virginia. InterNIC has two unrestricted WHOIS services: a WHOIS database of users related to the networking structure and operation of the Internet; and a general WAIS database, containing global white page-style listings of other users. WHOIS is accessed via Telnet, e-mail, Gopher, WAIS, and other WHOIS clients and tools.

Netfind. According to statistics, this tool is very reliable. It is able to find 5 million+ users located within more than 9,000 domains.

Finger. This can be used if the user knows a person's domain address. All that the user has to do is type finger user@domain or finger@domain to view a list of users who are logged on. It is often exploited to find weaknesses in a private network. Accordingly, most commercial sites decline Finger requests.

A more recent set of searching and indexing tools includes:

WebCrawler. This provides a high-quality, fast, and free Internet search service, freely available from America Online. Go to: http://webcrawler.com.

Yahoo!. This is a hierarchical subject-oriented guide for the world wide web and Internet. It categorizes sites under appropriate subjects. Go to: http://www.yahoo.com.

Alta Vista. Alta Vista claims to search through all the words at web and Usenet sites and ranks retrieval according to the frequency of the occurrences of the search words. Go to: http://www.altavista.digital.com.

Lycos. This is an excellent guide to the Internet, providing a catalog of URLs, a directory of the most popular sites, critical reviews of the web's top sites, real-time news links and so on. Go to: http://www.lycos.com.

InfoSeek. This is another free world wide web search service jointly offered by Infoseek, Netscape Communications, and Sun Microsystems Corporations. The service is accessed via Netscape's home page on the Internet. It is fast and accurate. Go to: http://info.infoseek.com.

There are several others. All these improved services make the WWW an easy environment to browse, even though it is the world's largest library of information online.

Real-Time Internet Conferencing

With a talk program, a user on one computer opens a split-screen session with a user on another system; each person sees what the other person types. Internet Relay Chat (IRC) and Multi-User Dimensions (MUDs) are two such programs that facilitate real-time communication over the Internet.

IRC takes place in real-time: Users join a channel and participate in one or more discussion(s). Most channels have specific discussion topics. If someone does not like the topics on existing channels, that person can create a new topic and invite others to join in. IRC FAQ located at http://www.kei.com/irc.html provides information on basic IRC operations, along with a list of servers. Further, it directs the reader to other appropriate sites for more information.

Today, Web-based conferencing on the Internet is now a common occurrence. For example, WebChat located at http://www.irsociety.com/webchat.html is used by corporations to produce live weekly interviews, sales presentations, Internet press conferences, and corporate teleconferencing with worldwide access at every user's local dial-up rate.

Another interesting web-based system is the Sociable Web that facilitates conference sessions in which users can insert hypertext links, sounds, and images as part of their discussion text. In this realm, Ubique Ltd.'s Virtual Places represents a commercial web-based conferencing product. It is a client/server software for real-time Internet conferencing that allows users to add graphics to discussions as well as converse by keyboard or by voice using a microphone.

MUDs allow real-time, text-based participation over the Internet. They are built around a variety of themes, fostering professional communities where scholars in a particular field collaborate. Depending on the theme on the MUD, different commands provide access to a wide variety of actions and speech techniques. To learn more about MUDs, the reader is urged to check out http://www.lysator.liu.se/mud/faq/faq1.html.

The World Wide Web (WWW)

WWW refers to a system that brings worldwide Internet resources together into a seamless, interactive environment where information is easily found and retrieved. It accomplishes this by using highlighted words that represent links to other documents. With clicks of a mouse, these links, referred to as the *hypertext links*, make it easy to navigate through material. They also allow a reviewer to make a comment, pose a question, or clarify a point by creating additional links without disturbing the integrity of the original discussion. For example, a user may receive documents that let him or her select *product sales* from a list of choices. The server could then produce another page with pictorial descriptions of the products, along with pricing, an e-mail address for a sales contact, and the option to download a complete catalog.

To carry out the various operations, a number of protocols are used. Hypertext Transfer Protocol (HTTP) governs the delivery of Hypertext along the Internet, and the Hypertext Markup Language (HTML) codes create and format a web document. Codes, called anchor codes, provide links within and between web documents and to other Internet protocols. If, for example, the user selects a catalog from the web page of a particular business, FTP will be invoked to send the catalog. For other requests, similar other protocols governing the respective facilities will come into play.

Facilitated by a client software called a browser, users can now open documents on hundreds of specific subjects. This software has transformed the web into a highly interactive environment where text, graphics, and even sound and video are supported. Thus, Hypertext is now a *hypermedia* environment that can be used for any number of things:

- Information and research
- Business and commercial useage
- Personal communication and self-expression
- Entertainment and social interaction

THE WEB BROWSERS

Hypertext-based browser, which typically resides within a user's desktop machine, is sometimes referred to as a client.

Mosaic is a browser, which was the precursor to the more advanced browsers used in today's Internet environment. This was placed in the public domain and was available free of charge from the National Center for Supercomputing Applications' (NCSA) Internet server. Mosaic relied on the TCP/IP communications protocols to retrieve files of information from server computers. If an enterprise allowed web requests to pass through their security firewall, Mosaic could retrieve data from computers located anywhere in the world. The retrieved file could be in text, video, or sound format. When first developed, businesses found such flexibility with format very appealing. People often referred to Mosaic as the web's "killer application," because early in its development cycle it made the Internet easy, powerful, and consistent across three desktop architectures, namely, PC, Macintosh, and workstations.

Netscape's *Navigator* is the popular client software for enterprise networks and the Internet. It represents more than 85 percent usage on the world wide web, according to a variety of the Internet sites such as The Internet Financial Database, The Scripps Research Institute, TISC, and the University of Illinois at Urbana-Champaign. The navigator provides a powerful environment for creating and maintaining live online applications for use within an enterprise or across the Internet. The applications include web browsing and collaboration features such as interactive electronic mail, integrated threaded discussion groups, and support for interactive multimedia content, such as embedded spreadsheets, animation, streaming audio and video, and 3-D capabilities.

Netscape *Navigator* Gold is the enhanced version of Netscape *Navigator*. It redefines the Internet client software standard by combining web exploring, e-mail, newsgroups, chat, and FTP capabilities with support for additional new features. Such new features facilitate improved ways of communicating and conducting business within and beyond the enterprise.

Bookmarks: Keeping Track of the Favorite Web Pages

Most web browsers offer a bookmark feature that can be used like an address book. The user adds, deletes, and organizes the Uniform Resource Locators (URLs), which refer to the addressing scheme for resources on the web, of his or her favorite web pages in the bookmark list, which can be organized into hierarchical categories. This hierarchical ordering is convenient for maintaining larger lists. Advanced bookmark software is also available that automatically monitors bookmarked sites for changes, eases the organization of bookmark files, and automates the export of bookmarks to HTML (web page) format. Smart-Marks offered by Netscape is a good example of such software. Refer to http://www.netscape.com.

Viewing Graphics with the Web Browser

A vast majority of graphic images on the web are in CompuServe's Graphic Interchange Format, commonly referred to as a GIF file. Or, they could be in a Joint Photographic Experts Group (JPEG) format. The web browser displays these images without any configuration requirement on the part of the user. However, there are other images that a web browser can handle only with the aid of additional software. Much of this software is freely available through the web. In addition to GIF and JPEG, Adobe's Portable Document Format and PostScript are also widely used. A partial list of popular graphic formats and their file extensions is provided below:

GIF	.gif	CompuServ's Graphic Interchange Format
JPEG	.jpg	Joint Photographic Expert's Format
PostScript	.ps	Adobe's PostScript
Portable Document Format	.pdf	Cross-platform PostScript subset
Macintosh Picture	.pic	Macintosh Picture Format

To view the Portable Document Format, it is necessary to download an Adobe Acrobat reader from http://www.adobe.com/Acrobat/. It is a free download.

Additionally, there may be occasions when one has to view a graphic image without the web browser or a document that happens to be in some other graphic format such as Tagged Image File Format (.tiff), or a Windows Bitmap (.bmp). In these situations, graphic viewer software such as PaintShop Pro or Graphic Workshop may be obtained through the web. The Usenet newsgroup: alt.binaries.pictures.d. provides excellent details on graphic images on the Internet.

Configuring the Web Browser for Sound and Video

Because standards for sound and video over the Internet are lacking, in order to hear audio clips and to see full-motion video over the web, one needs the software capable of dealing with the file format of a particular audio or video clip. Audio formats include:

Microsoft Waveform	.wav	Sound format standardized by Microsoft
Sun/Nextstep	.au, .snd	Sound format standardized by Sun/Nextstep
Mac/SGI	.aif	Sound format standardized by Macintosh
RealAudio	.ra, .ram	Sound format allowing real-time audio
MPEG Audio	.mp2	MPEG audio file
Sound Blaster	.sbi	Format for Sound Blaster sound card

RealAudio Player delivers voice data across the world wide web reliably and in real time over international connections or via capacity-constrained servers. It is available for free downloading (http://www.realaudio.com) over the Internet. For more information on audio formats, refer to ftp://rtfm.mit.edu/pub/usenet/news.answers/audio-fmts.

Following are formats for full motion video on the web:

MPEG	.mpg	Full motion video similar to JPEG format
Audio Video Interleave	.avi	Microsoft's video format
Quicktime Movie	.mov	Apple's video format
Digital Video Interactive	.dvi	Full motion video
FLI	.fli	Full motion video

As in audio clips, one must use software capable of dealing with the video clip. This software includes VMPEG, Xing MPEG, vfwrun, Quicktime Viewer, and AAPLAY. Readers are urged to visit: http://www.travelresource.com/help.html. This site maintains a dictionary of the different file formats with direct links to the software utilities needed to convert or play the files.

Interactive Applications: HotJAVA and Web Browser Plug-Ins

In 1996, another exciting innovation on the Internet was transforming static web pages into an interactive online application development environment. An object-oriented application development language called Java, which allows users online interactivity over the web, was introduced.

Java is now well entrenched in the Internet environment. Java helps web page designers build and run mini-applications called applets, which users download and run on their desktops. These applets, if properly designed, are quite versatile. For example, they can automatically update stock prices in real time, or show a video clip of a new product to a customer complete with updated price information and order entry forms. Netscape, the owner of Netscape Navigator (the web browser with the largest market share), is incorporating HotJava technology into the latest version of their web browsers. This bodes well for the future of Java. For information on Java programming, Java applets, and HotJava, the following sites are recommended:

Java Programming	http://www.gamelan.com/Gamelan.programming.html
Java Bibliography	http://www.rpi.edu/~decemj/works/java/bib.html
Wild World HotJava	http://www.science.wayne.edu/~joey/java.html

Along with the introduction of Java comes the web browser plug-ins, which are another significant milestone in the evolution of the Internet environment. The Netscape Navigator web browser has a functionality-enhancing feature that provides for inline support for a huge range of Live Objects. With Live Objects, developers are able to deliver rich multimedia content through Internet sites, thereby allowing users to view that content effortlessly with plug-ins such as Adobe Acrobat, Apple QuickTime, and Macromedia Shockwave for Director in the client window. All this is possible without launching any other external helper applications. Netscape Navigator plug-ins include:

- Acrobat Amber Reader by Adobe
- QuickTime by Apple Computers
- RealAudio by Progressive Networks
- Shockwave for Director by Macromedia and several others.

These can be accessed through Netscape Communications Homepage (http://www.netscape.com).

Microsoft (http://www.microsoft.com) has also created a development environment called Blackbird that enables developers to write online interactive applications on the web. The success of Microsoft Network and Microsoft's Internet Explorer has a bearing on the success of Blackbird.

Both Java and Blackbird have another competitor: WebObjects created by NeXT (http://www.next.com). It is more portable in that it runs on Windows NT, Solaris Sun OS, HP-UX, Digital's UNIX, and NeXT's MachOS. WebObjects has simplified the programming required to create interactive web pages.

Virtual Reality and the World Wide Web: It's Here Now

Virtual reality systems create three-dimensional computer-generated simulations to provide sensations that emulate real-world activities. Currently, there are wide ranging applications of virtual reality that include computer-aided design (CAD), medical diagnosis, scientific experimentation, flight simulation, and entertainment, especially 3-D video games. The most widely used industrial virtual reality application is CAD. Engineers are the primary users of this application, since they test computerized 3-D models of products by entering the models themselves and examining and manipulating parts from all angles.

The use of a Virtual Reality Modeling Language (VRML)-enhanced web-browser would permit one to experience virtual reality on the Internet. VRML is an open standard that defines a three-dimensional object, assigns a location to that object, and manipulates the perspective to view the object. Further, the VRML standard provides specifications for making a useful link to another Internet site, putting colors and textures on objects, and showing where the lights are. WebFX is a free Netscape plug-in that serves as a VRML browser, allowing the user to move through 3-D world at web sites with VRML pages.

CHAPTER 2

Two Themes of Satellite-Based Internet Use

Theme 1: Internet-Based Project Management

The more effectively an organization can manage project details, control costs, allocate and manage project resources, and adhere to an optimized schedule, the more competitive and profitable the organization will be.

To maximize project management success, it is crucial for the entire project team to maximize access to up-to-date project information. Site-based project managers need ready access to schedules, resource allocation information, Request For Information (RFI), material deliveries, unresolved issues, and activity status updates for their particular projects. Professional planners and schedulers in the home office need up-to-date information on costs, schedules, material and resource allocations, and activity status information for all ongoing projects.

With these requirements in mind, Internet-based project management provides a structured, integrated, fully scalable solution for coordinating people, teams, and projects distributed throughout an enterprise. Internet-based project management solutions provide a unified environment in which project or contract administrators in the field or in the home office can integrate project management software packages to control contracts, drawings, and changes and correspondence associated with projects.[1] These software packages enable managers at all levels to stay current on submittals and transmittals, materials delivery, and RFIs and help to ensure the planned schedule is executed to an on-time, on-budget completion.

Inasmuch as all the software solutions have been built around a common project management architecture, managers throughout an organization can use the software tools that best support their tasks, to access whatever project information they need in order to plan and act effectively. Internet-based project management solutions are designed to maximize the effectiveness of the entire project team through a combination of efficient, compatible tools and easy access to shared, up-to-date information.[2] Figure 2.1 provides an illustration of one such solution offered by Primavera, which represents a high-end project management software.* The figure depicts a Project Home Page, which normally will have linkage to a database of work in progress and secured from nonauthorized personnel. This section may contain the field reports specifications, financial reporting, time sheets, and even the latest AutoCAD drawings using DXF (Drawing Interchange [eXchange] Format)/DWG (AutoCAD drawing, or older generic CADD drawing format). This provides a forum for inexpensive and immediate communication between distant team members.[3]

Project managers can remotely monitor work in progress, and the project team can improve customer relations by allowing clients access to the appropriate Project Pages, keeping them constantly updated on project status. In addition, Internet technology allows the project team to access global Internet resources for research. For instance, the team can use Virtual Reality Modeling Language (VRML) to review plans to eliminate oversights caused by 2D plans. As both a communication and a research tool, the Internet can improve productivity and profitability.

Increasingly, organizations throughout the industry are pushing more responsibility for project management into the field. Organizations that distribute project management responsibilities in this way can gain

---

* Permission to quote and reproduce tables, charts, and other materials for this chapter has been kindly granted by Semaphone Interactive, Netmosphere, and Primavera Systems, Inc.

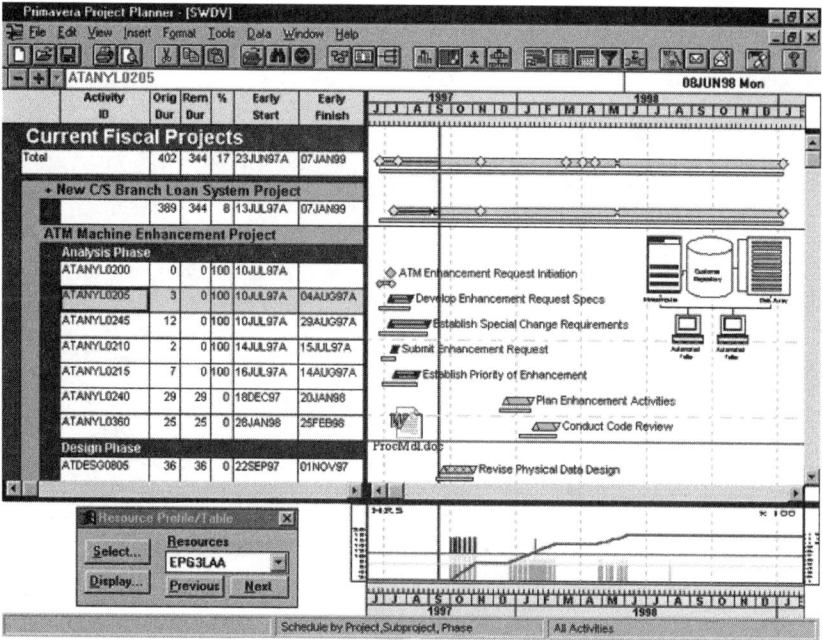

Figure 2.1 Sample Project Home Page for Managing Multiple Projects in a Multi-User Environment

Source: Primavera, http://www.primavera.com/PRODUCTS/p3win.html

significant benefits: On-site project managers can respond more quickly to issues arising on site, they can see the immediate effects of changes and delays on project deadlines, and they can make better decisions because of the tools to which they have access.

If an organization uses the Internet-based project management model, project management professionals in the home office can play an oversight role. With multi-user, server-based software tools, managers in the home office can gather and analyze remote project information to provide senior management with a timely, accurate, and consolidated view of all ongoing projects. Companies gain an increased ability to plan and schedule effectively, to oversee change, to manage contract responsibilities and details, and to know the exact status of all projects at any given time. Figure 2.2 provides a sample of a project tracking software tool.

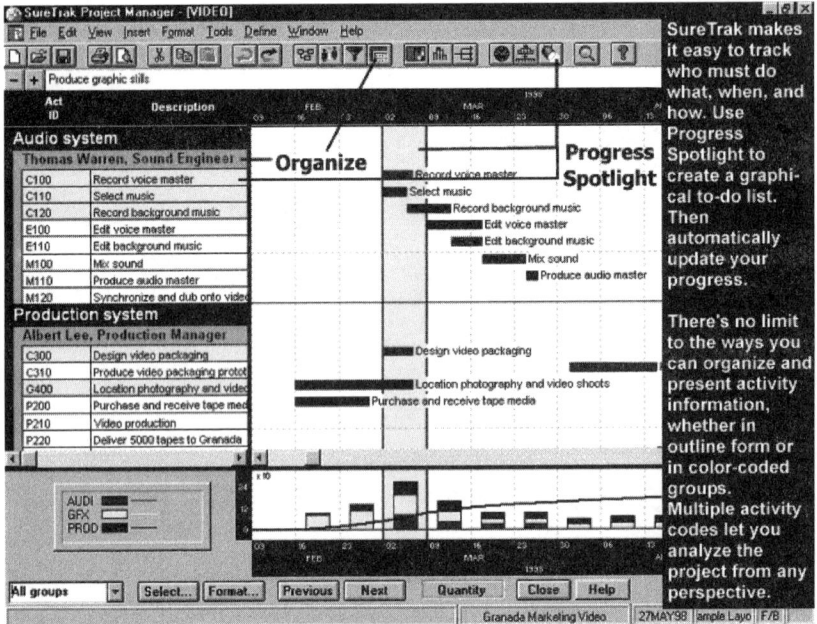

Figure 2.2 Updating, Analyzing and Forecasting with Project Management Software

Source: Primavera, http://www.primavera.com/products/stwin.html

Unless the organization uses project management tools that conform to an integrated architecture that provides the necessary structure, common rules and data definitions, and well-defined conduits through which project information can easily and accurately be shared, the organization gains none of these advantages. Without a simple, well-defined way to share project information between the field and the home office, the organization is vulnerable to an overall loss of management control, a loss that threatens to compromise both the organization's profitability and its ability to compete effectively in the marketplace.

Internet-based project management is not a radical departure from time-tested and proven project management approaches. Indeed, Internet-based project management simply maps the best practices in project management to the multi-project, multi-site organization and supports that organization with an integrated set of tools that properly reflect the project and managerial relationships in that organization.

In essence, Internet-based project management represents a structured, integrated, and scalable solution for coordinating people, teams, and projects. The qualifying terms in this definition—*structured, integrated,* and *scalable*—are critical. The organization that attempts to implement a project management solution which does not reflect these qualifications will be unable to manage projects effectively.

Structure

Project managers understand that projects are all about structure—the structure and foundation that support the physical project itself, as well as the structure of how the project is defined and managed. Effective project management relies on consistent use of work breakdown structures, repeatable processes, and dependable ways of communicating results and changes. To perform effectively, all project management tools need to work together. They must share common data definitions and structures. They must share an understanding of how relationships are defined between activities and costs and resources. Similar to an accounting system, an Internet-based project management system provides definitions, rules and conventions, ways of doing things, and ways of communicating.

For the planner in the home office or the manager overseeing very large projects, an Internet-based project management solution can provide access to the software tools preferred by the most sophisticated project professionals in the business environment. Figure 2.3 depicts the processes embedded in such software tools. The use of such embedded process architecture makes it easier to insert activities, rearrange them, and put them in sequence to model the flow of work. Through the Trace Logic, project planners can review the sequence of activities, so they can easily see how the downstream effect of changes and delays will affect the rest of the project.

For project managers handling smaller projects or overseeing projects on a part-time basis, the Internet-based project management solution can also provide access to other software tools that might be needed by managers who do not require extensive multi-project capabilities. Although specialized software packages are designed to support different roles, different applications, and different kinds of projects, they work

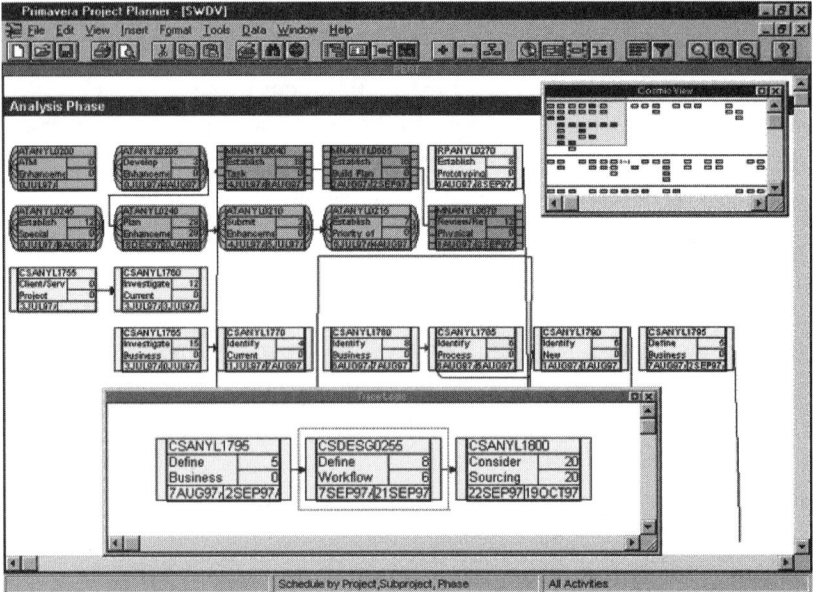

Figure 2.3 Projects at a Glance with PERT View

Source: Primavera, http://www.primavera.com/products/stwin_feat.html

together to provide the foundation for an effective, results-driven implementation of Internet-based project management. This foundation is reinforced with appropriate links among multiple projects and common resource pools, such as shared activity codes, specifications, contacts, and cost codes. This shared structure allows individual projects within a shared database to be compared and summarized; without it, it is impossible to assemble the details of multiple, diverse projects into a meaningful overall picture.

Integration

Although a common structure enables managers to work with information captured or created in other software driven project management applications, effective management of multiple projects requires more than just a common structure. It requires the easy integration of information from multiple project plans. From a business standpoint, no project is truly isolated from all the others. If the equipment in use on one project is not available for use on a second project, the schedule for that second project is at risk. That, in turn, could cause problems for a third or fourth project. Eliminating this risk requires the integration of these diverse schedules.

Internet-based project management provides the integration that enables managers throughout the enterprise to determine how schedules and events impact other ongoing projects. Just as relationships between activities can be defined in an individual project plan, Internet-based project management solutions enable project managers to identify relationships and dependencies between project plans created and managed independently by project managers in different geographical locations. Instead of a change in one plan precipitating a cascading set of unanticipated problems in other plans, managers throughout the enterprise can be instantly informed of the initial change and take steps to manage their individual projects effectively in response.

Because Internet-based project management incorporates the powerful contract control features of other software packages, all managers are made aware of issues and dependencies on reviews and approvals. Managers know who is responsible for pending decisions and actions. By early identification of potential problems or delays and sharing this information with project schedulers, managers can help to keep the project on schedule.

Scalability

The third key to a successful project management solution is scalability. Projects vary in size, shape, and scope. Some are huge and require sophisticated planning; professionals dedicated to the project control these. Status checks and progress updates are performed on an ongoing basis. Analysis is performed repeatedly to confirm project progress and identify problems in order to make corrections.

For smaller projects, managers limit their project management responsibilities, with only a few hours per week devoted to project updating and reporting. These managers need a basic knowledge of scheduling, easy-to-use software tools, and the occasional availability of experienced project managers for advice. Individually, many software packages can support everything from the smallest of projects worthy of management attention to the largest of projects. Together, they can support everything from a small organization with only a few small projects to a large enterprise with hundreds of projects underway throughout the world. Moreover, the architecture of Internet-based project management enables an organization to continuously add projects to its portfolio without compromising the efficacy of its project management system.

Companies that standardize on a single software solution—a "one-size-fits-all" approach—risk over-complicating or underpowering their project personnel. With Internet-based project management, the manager's project tools are scaled to the size and scope of the project and to the skills and requirements of the project manager.

THE BENEFITS

Four benefits emerge from the Internet-based approach to project management: *coordination, communication, empowerment,* and *competitive advantage*. These benefits are almost impossible to realize if an organization implements a solution that is not coherently structured, integrated, or scalable.

Coordination

In an Internet-based project management environment, there are no unimportant projects. Every project becomes visible and every project team knows that it must continuously evaluate performance and provide updates. This visibility ensures integrity in reporting, and forces project schedulers, project managers, and even senior management to be aware of how projects are progressing.

Communication

The project team implicitly understands that its biggest challenge is keeping all members headed in the same direction. In an Internet-based project management environment, a project that veers off course is immediately noticed, and managers can take quick, effective action to bring the project back in line. Internet-based project management facilitates the necessary dialogue among project managers by directing attention to issues, problems, and assumptions so they can be examined and clarified.

Empowerment

Power and confidence flourish when the individuals on-site understand their roles in the context of the overall picture. The Internet-based project management model empowers members with the knowledge that they are in sync with the organization's objectives because it emphasizes how every piece fits into the whole. Moreover, Internet-based project management exposes priorities, commitments, and dependencies. A solid understanding of what is expected and when enables each member of the project team to act with confidence.

Competitive Advantage

Internet-based project management promotes good decision making. Managers can assess project costs and benefits. When alternatives must be considered and choices made, Internet-based project management provides reliable tools to guide time-sensitive decision making. Internet-based project management enables professionals in various industries—engineering, construction, architecture, utilities, information systems and technology, R&D, manufacturing—to meet schedule and budget commitments, even when commitments are aggressive (which positions the enterprise to compete more effectively and more profitably in the marketplace).

INTERNET-BASED PROJECT MANAGEMENT IN ACTION

Internet-based project management involves linking people and projects to facilitate flawless project execution and optimal results. It is more than a set of complementary tools for developing and managing schedules. Because it links the contract and communications management features of one type of software package with the powerful planning, control, and reporting features of other software packages, Internet-based project management provides project managers throughout the organization with a uniquely comprehensive perspective on projects.

Stand-alone software packages cannot provide as comprehensive a picture. They cannot reflect how the inevitable changes, the approval process, or the unforeseen submittals which occur in every project affect the schedule, because they lack the seamless integration available from the Internet medium.

The Internet-based project management solution provides an environment in which a project manager can use the tool that is most appropriate for his or her skill level and that best suits the nature and scope of the project at hand. At the same time, it provides for integration of information created and managed by various applications, which in turn facilitates the overall management of projects throughout the enterprise. Figure 2.4 illustrates how the Internet web page helps build and

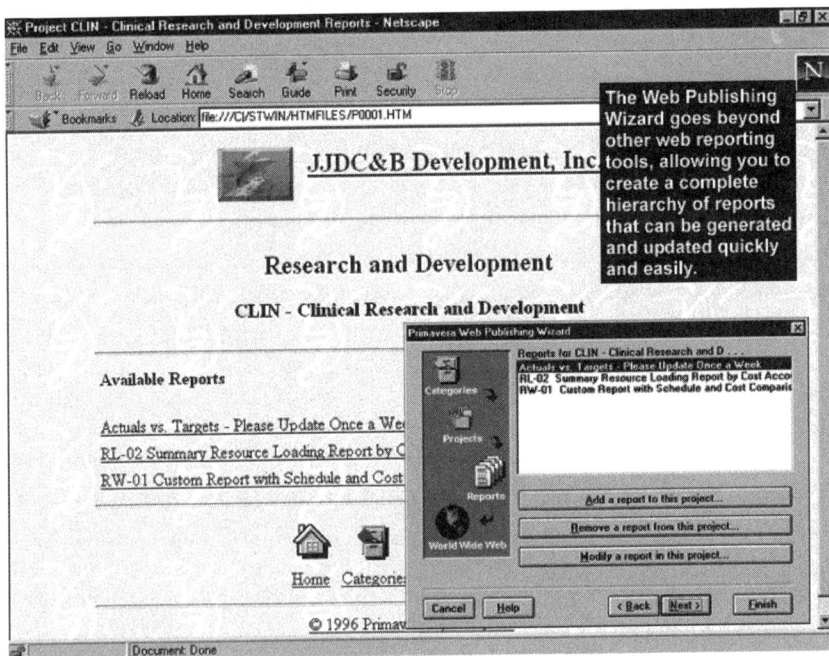

Figure 2.4 Internet Web Pages Containing Up-to-Date Project Reports and Links to Related Files

Source: Primavera, http://www.primavera.com/artwork/screens/webwiz2.gif

maintain structured web pages containing up-to-date project reports and links to related files.

Because of the links available through the Internet web site, communication is no longer a problem. Now, team members know what to do and when—at their convenience, without the conflicting demands of several project managers and functional managers overseeing different activities at different times.[4] Figure 2.5 illustrates the situation without an Internet web site, whereas Figure 2.6 depicts the improvement possible with the Internet web server.

Figure 2.5 shows that project managers spend most of their time doing project administration instead of resolving project issues. Often they devote an inordinate amount of time calling and e-mailing the project members to learn the status of assigned tasks and milestones, so that the schedule can be updated frequently. This iterative task prohibits them from attempting to resolve issues that might threaten the success of the project.[5]

The improvement made possible by the Internet web server, as illustrated in Figure 2.6, is a simple case of storing projects and resources centrally so that:

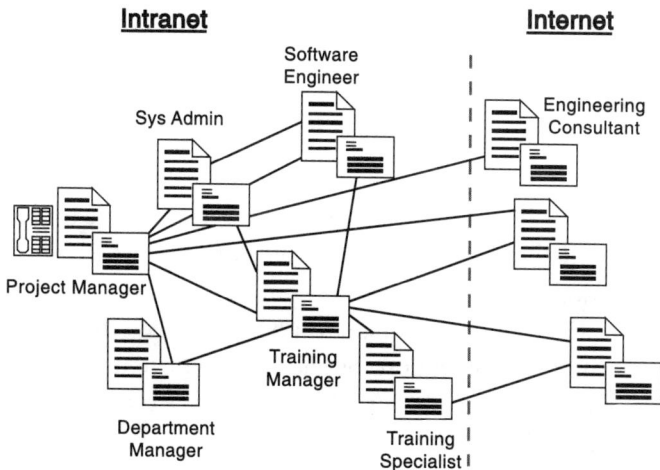

Figure 2.5 Project Management without an Internet Web Site

Source: Netmosphere White Papers,
http://www.netmosphere.com/actionplay/whitepapers/index.html

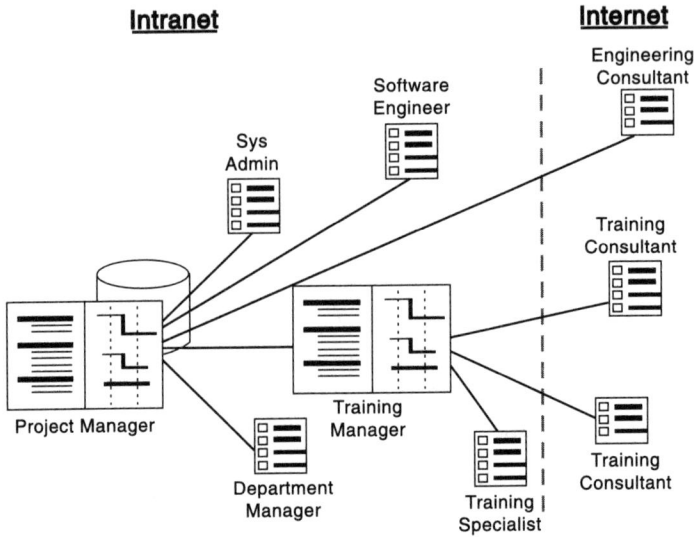

Figure 2.6 Project Management with the Aid of an Internet Web Server

Source: Netmosphere White Papers,
http://www.netmosphere.com/actionplay/whitepapers/index.html

- Team members can access projects regardless of their physical location.
- Project managers can properly allocate resources across multiple projects.
- Milestones can be shared across projects.

Under this improved condition, project managers are able to spend their time completing tasks and resolving issues instead of querying status and revising schedules.[6]

Once a project plan is complete and published, the Internet web allows two-way communication, providing an efficient turnaround of a project's status. Team members see the detailed activity codes for each assignment for a clear understanding of what is expected. As the completed tasks are checked off, the sample master schedule shown in Figure 2.7 is updated in real time, allowing each member to see the very latest schedule information. With that vital up-to-date information, project team members are able to make crucial decisions with confidence.[7]

Project start & finish dates

Task & milestone list

Exported tasks

Task resource

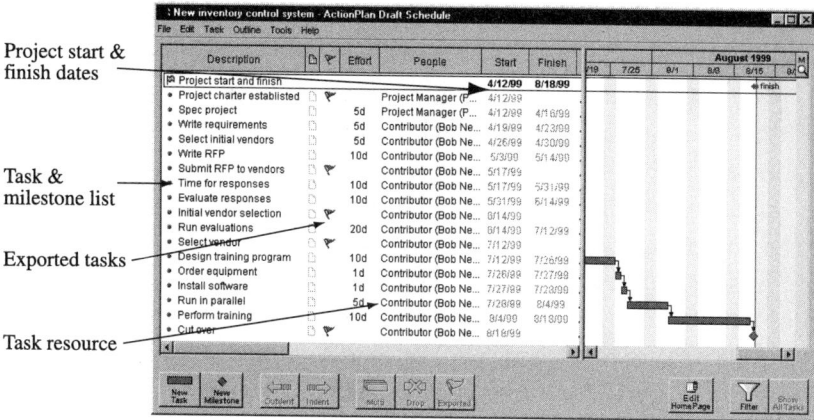

Figure 2.7 Up-to-the-Minute Information Via the Internet Web

Source: Netmosphere White Papers,
http://www.netmosphere.com/actionplan/whitepapers/index.html

Internet-based project management is the key to successful project management in today's global business environment. That theme is explored through case studies in Chapters 3 through 6.

Theme 2: Project Management for Internet Businesses

The Internet is fundamentally unbalanced: for one click of a mouse button that sends a 30- to 50-character web address, the response from the destination server at the far end can vary from 25 to 700K of web page information, with text, hypertext, images, and possibly audio and video thrown in for good measure. If the one web click is multiplied by 100, 1,000, or 10,000, the reality of Internet Service Provider (ISP) business problems sets in. The communication links become overloaded, National Access Points (NAPs) become congested, and popular web servers, such as the Mars Path Finder Mission, become overburdened. Until recently, many ISPs thought larger leased lines would remedy the situation; however, experience shows that larger leased lines do not necessarily satisfy their business needs. Instead, with greater deployment of

ISDN, cable modems, and xDSL services that increase bandwidth into the home, ISPs are witnessing ever-increasing strains.[8]

To manage their businesses more cost-effectively, ISPs are exploring another technology option. Caching, or storing frequently accessed information on a local server, eases the burden on overloaded leased lines. ISPs can maintain local cache boxes, and popular web pages and other information can be stored in them, rather than requesting and receiving the same copy of information from the origin server each time. With one copy of the most popular information stored locally, ISPs offer web surfers faster response time. Web surfers or end users retrieve information from across the ISPs' local area network and avoid being routed through multiple hops across an NAP to a heavily loaded web server. In this scenario, ISPs dramatically reduce the traffic load down through their leased-links to the backbone and avoid the expense of adding additional connections.

Several companies are building large terabyte-sized community caches positioned at NAPs. In theory, these community caches provide localized means for an ISP cache to be updated in a small number of hops. Local caches pull down updates through a traditional leased-line connection. Problems arise when the community cache itself becomes a bottleneck for local cache updating, as local caches communicate with it at an NAP. Similarly, the community cache will generate a large amount of traffic to ensure that its copies of information are the most current.

To avoid these bottlenecks and further streamline the ISP business environment, Doug Humphrey, who started DIGEX in 1992 and eventually sold it to a telephone company, has developed a scheme that alters Internet architecture forever. There is no new technology involved; instead, his new venture proposes to move the web traffic via satellite to caching disks at local ISPs.[9] The ISP leases a turnkey box with the hardware, software, and the satellite receiver from Humphrey. The box uses Internet Caching Protocol, which makes it a handy attachment for any existing cache, and fits together with other caching products. All the usual processes, including the caller's request of a particular page and the local cache's routine to verify that the requested page is onboard, and then to retrieve the page from the origin server if required, now occur at a much faster pace.[10] Humphrey's scheme will provide an additional service in that an advisory notice will indicate that the requested web page has arrived over the Net at his own big cache server. The big cache server retrieves the end-user requested page from the real web site and uses a 2 Mbps satellite link to send the page out to the disk surface of all the other ISP caches that are equipped with small-dish receivers.[11]

The interface between satellite and web cache creates many improvements in the ISP's business. First, the ISPs become part of a much larger cache community—as big as the total user base of all ISPs subscribing to the service. Second, the ISPs receive additional web pages that reach their equipment without traveling through congested leased-line connections to the backbone. The pages arrive at the local ISP caches via satellite free of charge. The cumulative user base of all participating ISPs now becomes the community and impacts the "hit rate."

The basic premise of hit rate is that a small ISP with a web cache and 1,500 subscribers would be doing well if that ISP can shunt 10 to 12 percent of the web page requests to its cache. A larger ISP with 5,000 customers might be in the 16 to 18 percent range. America On Line (AOL), with approximately 10 million customers, can achieve hit rates in excess of 60 percent. Translated into the ISP's business performance requirements, higher hit rate means customer satisfaction, since customers receive a fast response with current versions of the particular pages.[12]

With Doug Humphrey's plans to collocate every web server at every subscribing ISP where the callers are, the web no longer needs to travel through the backbone. This scheme scales exceptionally well. If three, four, or five ISPs use it, it works. If 5,000 of them use it, the performance is greatly improved. In a case study presented in Chapter 5, the rationale becomes more apparent. The primary focus here is to highlight the project management benefit for the Internet businesses.

Several people are currently evaluating the prospect of attaching the receivers at various hub cities connected to a backbone, since they believe Humphrey's scheme could work equally well at a backbone. ISPs not directly subscribing to Humphrey's services, yet connected to the receivers, would still carry the traffic on their connection to the backbone, but the page would arrive much faster without ever transiting through the core. This suggests that the Internet backbone is about to change from being a data transmission service to a signaling system that carries tiny flows to request web pages, record hits and statistical information, and signal between caches. The backbone will continue to carry e-mail and file transfer protocol, which represent small percentages of the Net flow.

This is happening at a time when the interest in carrying voice over the Internet is strong, since it promises to be one of the most profitable opportunities for the ISPs. Every major player has a product, but to carry voice, the web traffic must be taken out or reduced substantially. Humphrey's satellite-based scheme offers the possibility of doing that. Satellite topologies complement broadcasting attributes and are largely unencumbered by the infrastructure that terrestrial Internet traffic must navigate. Satellite is ready to move ahead of the terrestrial world by delivering and distributing databases and large software, including streaming audio and video. Satellite datacasting is a fast-moving business offering a very different Internet architecture to ease the increasing demand on bandwidth coming from many new applications. That is no small concern to ISPs. They want to increase their business by cashing in on the unlimited growth potential of the Internet and Internet-based telecommunications services, thereby improving their bottom line.[13] Chapter 5 examines the current industry outlooks in case studies of Doug Humphrey's and other similar ventures.

PART II

CASE STUDIES

CHAPTER 3

Manufacturing and the Internet

Today, in virtually every industry, firms of all sizes exchange large technical data files, transmit orders and specifications to trading partners, and give potential customers access to electronic catalogs. As a business tool, the Internet has proved to be invaluable for these exchanges. However, the speed at which bits may race to their destination to be reassembled into words or images is not sufficient to judge the Internet. The important question to ask is how these technical capabilities can make the enterprise and its employees more efficient and more responsive to their customers.

Today's competitive environment has forced many companies to consider joint projects in which:

- Companies form alliances rapidly and easily to produce new products and employ advanced manufacturing concepts.
- "Software system brokers" connect users who need temporary access to sophisticated manufacturing tools that would normally be too expensive to acquire.
- Manufacturers and suppliers use "intelligent" procurement systems to facilitate and accelerate parts procurement, billing, and payment transactions in order to reduce costs, improve accuracy, and meet customer demand in a timely manner.

Because the reach of the Internet is wide and the transaction cost of the network is low, large, medium, and small companies are investigating "virtual alliances" with other trading partners, as well as project management applications to meet these imperatives.

Manufacturing Management

To manage projects effectively in a manufacturing enterprise, the environment must be completely understood. Manufacturing encompasses several functions that must be strategically planned, organized, scheduled, controlled, and terminated.[1] Although it is beyond the scope of this section to provide complete coverage of all these functions, numerous operations within the planning, organizing, scheduling, and control functions of project management can be identified and differentiated to understand a manufacturing cycle. These include forecasting, inventory control, process planning, machine sequencing, quality control, decision analysis, production planning, cost analysis, process control, facility layout, work analysis, and a host of other functions.[2]

To be successfully managed, each of these functions or operations must be viewed as a critical project whose success relies on an effective project management technique. The focus of this chapter is to bring project management techniques to bear on the operational aspects of manufacturing activities. For the purpose of this chapter, we refer to discrete parts manufacturing industries as "manufacturing." These industries encompass everything from automobile and computer products to wood furniture. Today, discrete parts manufacturers face intense competition that threatens their very survival. One of their basic functional requirements to stay competitive is to *improve productivity*.[3] Toward that end, manufacturers are extending the enterprise by using systems that have been at the forefront in integrating the "information silos" of individual production and distribution functions. These systems typically include applications in project management, materials resources planning (MRP), master production scheduling, financials, and accounting.

Today's manufacturing environment is characterized by an explosion in requirements for linking business processes, timeliness, and access.[4] To meet these requirements, manufacturers must move from mere integration of information silos into adopting a new generation of technology based on advanced planning systems. The underlying strength of the advanced planning system is that it empowers small and medium-sized manufacturers by integrating business with the latest and best information from everyone involved in the manufacturing enterprise.[5]

Software applications contributing to advanced planning include forecasting, customer-interaction software, distribution management, production planning, warehouse and transportation planning, and supply-chain optimization. The software enables managers to find opportunities for improvements far beyond what even the most experienced manager can glean through intuition.

With advanced planning systems, a manufacturing enterprise can plan across the total range of an enterprise's activity and then gradually adjust to optimize results. However, this presupposes an infrastructure that can consolidate data concerning disparate processes: materials sourcing from different suppliers, manufacturing in different parts of the world, and output packaging and distribution.[6]

Evolution of Infrastructure for Manufacturing Management Applications

Enterprise resources planning (ERP) is the generic term for integrated systems that automate and integrate business processes found in manufacturing environments, including business processes occurring on plant production floors. ERP is increasingly seen as a transaction backbone and data source for ancillary, decision-support systems that use memory-based processing to perform rapid "what-if?" simulations. These simulations determine the best quantity of product to produce and select the least expensive method of providing flexibility in capacity while measuring production requirements.[7] Typically this involves:

1. *Forecasting* to predict levels of weekly or monthly product activity typically over one to two years.
2. *Advanced planning* to target production over months or years using constraint models that treat both materials and capacity. Frequently, these systems download data from ERP to a dedicated

server that does memory-resident processing for fast replanning or for evaluating alternative production scenarios. The results can eventually be reintegrated with the transactional business application systems.

3. *Dynamic scheduling* to deal with short-term production schedules, typically a few days to a few weeks of production. A system can specify the detailed execution of the production plan generated by an advanced planning system, taking into account the most current plant-floor conditions. Also, the systems can be used on a stand-alone basis. The schedules specify a sequence in which work is to proceed, based on available capacity.

4. *Demand/distribution management* to optimize quantities of each product to be made at each plant and to be distributed to each warehouse such that manufacturing and distribution costs are minimized and customer demand is met.

5. *Warehouse management* to integrate work performed within warehouses and distribution centers by means of an execution system for distribution. Basic strategies are to increase throughput and productivity by managing the full range of warehouse resources. These strategies supplant simple storage and retrieval of materials.

6. *Transportation and logistics* to support warehouse management. Integration between the two is increasingly common. Whether using transportation systems from a supply-chain vendor or outsourcing logistics planning and management to a third-party provider, managers are striving to optimize distribution facilities.

To reiterate the point, ERP provides a single interface for managing all the activities performed in manufacturing. The more recent ERP systems have added new functions that address customer interaction and management of relationships with suppliers and vendors, thereby making the systems more up-to-date and externally oriented. Vendors are working with other small to medium-sized vendors to make ERP more useful and acceptable, particularly in the area of implementations, which can cost more than the software licenses. ERP has played a critical role in getting small and medium-sized manufacturers to focus on facilitating business process changes across the enterprise. By linking multiple plants and distribution facilities, ERP solutions have facilitated a change in thinking that has its ultimate expression in the extended enterprise and better management.

Two modules within ERP in particular are responsible for production planning and execution. These are the master production schedule (MPS) and material resource planning (MRP). The MPS outlines the production plan for all units, based on forecasts and orders, whereas the MRP module translates the master schedule into individual, time-phased component requirements.

According to experts in inventory and materials management, the major weaknesses of this type of system include:

1. The assumption that lead times are known constants
2. The system requires fixed routings
3. The sequencing logic prioritizes orders only by period or date
4. All work is loaded under assumption of infinite capacity
5. The process of regeneration is time-consuming

No single technology can overcome all these weaknesses. Unless these issues are addressed, the present-day project management in a manufacturing enterprise could hardly be considered useful and efficient. The solution calls for different solver technologies that must be carefully chosen, based on the problem to be solved.[8] It is hoped that readers can learn by examples.

Many recent studies indicate that the design process exerts the greatest influence on a product's life cycle: Approximately 60 percent of a product's cost is fixed early in the design process. An Institute for Defense Analysis report noted that advanced manufacturing techniques that enable the rapid exchange of information not only increase quality and reduce the number of design changes by 50 percent, but also reduce total costs by 30 to 60 percent, development time by 35 to 60 percent, design and product defects by 30 to 80 percent, and scrap work by 58 to 75 percent.

For example, Intel Corporation used computer-based concurrent engineering and improved communication among design teams to provide simulation, consistency, and the sharing of data among concurrent work teams. This process improvement reduced the time from design-to-sample in half, even though product complexity had doubled. The company also achieved a 95 percent success rate on the first silicon fabrication of new products. These successes enabled Intel Corporation to retain 95 percent of the flash memory market even in the face of strong Japanese competition.

Implementation of proprietary concurrent engineering systems has allowed Japanese automakers to decrease time-to-market for new cars by more than 30 percent, enabling them to gain considerable market share and to increase pressure on U.S. automakers.

The CALS Contractor Integrated Technical Information Service (CITIS): Business Case Feasibility Study evaluated the impact of a common data management, storage, retrieval, and exchange service for transferring contractor design and manufacturing data among the Air Force and its B2 subcontractors. The savings included a 5.4 percent reduction in the total B2 spares dollars, a 23 percent reduction in modification lead time, a 1.8 percent increase in the average availability of aircraft fleet, and a 90 percent reduction in the contractor data submittals. Estimated total cost savings ranged from $536 million to $894 million, for investments that ranged from $9 million to $30 million.

Harley-Davidson used just-in-time inventory control and total quality management practice to reduce manufacturing cycle time for motorcycle frames from 72 days to just 2 days. The company also improved final product quality from 50 percent to 99 percent.

Using the same productivity improvement programs, Digital Equipment Corporation reduced overall inventory from 16 weeks to 3 weeks, and its defect rate dropped from 17 percent to 3 percent. 3M also experienced a 70-fold reduction in critical defects, appearance defects, and packaging problems.

The French automobile manufacturer PSA Peugeot Citroen succeeded in creating closer, more efficient ties with its many suppliers and implementing just-in-time inventory control. They used an electronic communications network, ODETTE (Organization of Data Exchange via Tele Transmission in Europe). It improved inventory turnover by nearly 40 percent, reduced the number of unassembled cars on the line by 70 percent, and provided customers with a choice of nearly 30 percent more models. The company increased the quality of its products and customer satisfaction levels, as evidenced by its departure from a monthly order cycle to a multi-day one.

Simpson Industries (Plymouth, Michigan) is a first-tier supplier of just-in-time, high-quality parts to the Big Three automotive manufacturers. The company provides power train and chassis components designed to cope with problematic noise vibration and harsh environments, as well as modular systems such as fuel and water pumps. Simpson must operate under extremely short interval lead times for actual manufacture and shipment of goods.

Simpson has applied an integrated manufacturing solution from Denver-based J. D. Edwards that empowers the company to plan capacity, proactively schedule production, and communicate more efficiently with key customers and suppliers. With this system implementation, which includes an IBM Global Service supported RISC-based AS/400 technical infrastructure facilitating seamless communications with customers and suppliers on a 7 × 24 basis, Simpson has improved its status as a member of a major automotive supply chain. Electronic data interchange (EDI) between Simpson and the Big Three has improved dramatically, thereby impacting logistics. When Simpson ships a truck to Chrysler, GM, or any other customer, the company must notify them within a short period of time that trucks are en route, what the parts numbers are, and how many there are.

Before the system implementation, Simpson's effectiveness rating on this key shipment notification metric ranged from 92 percent to 96 percent; after system implementation, the rating has risen to 99.9 percent. Table 3.1 lists several other recent solver technologies that are transforming manufacturing operations.

From these trends one can infer that manufacturers, irrespective of their sizes, are developing and implementing advanced automated technologies to increase the speed of design and production and to reduce costs. Although the solutions have been accomplished with a high degree of sophistication, they tend to focus mostly on discrete manufacturing operations.

To remain competitive, many large enterprises, such as Boeing, General Motors, Ford, Newport News Shipbuilding, Caterpillar, and Intel invest in innovative programs that focus on achieving integration

Table 3.1 Moving Toward Long-Term Partnerships*

Software Developers	Solver Technologies
Frontier	A fully integrated software solution for multimode discrete manu facturing operations. With one of the largest installed bases of to-order manufacturers, Frontier provides a configuration-based business tool integrated with its manufacturing, distribution, and financial systems. Frontier will include quoting & estimating, service and warranty, sales automation, truck scheduling, purchasing, and logistics.
MOVEX	MOVEX helps improve manufacturers' and distributors' business performances by streamlining manufacturing, distribution, financial, and executive performance management processes. Specific MOVEX industry solutions include: make-to-order, furniture, apparel, food & beverage, pulp & paper, electronics, pharmaceutical, and industrial equipment. Available in 24 languages.
ERPx	ERPx is an integrated system of manufacturing software that manages manufacturing planning and execution functions. Features include online, real-time posting of add, change, delete; online item search; full-screen maintenance capability; multiplant and multibranch capabilities; product costing; paperless MPS/MRP; capacity requirements planning and full capabilities for inventory management, purchasing, sales order processing including configuration management, and sales forecasting.
VISUAL	VISUAL offers such special make-to-stock features as standard costing, master scheduling, and rough-cut capacity planning. VISUAL meets the needs of manufacturers that standard MRP packages do not—e.g., fully integrated finite scheduling of materials and resources, actual costing, purchasing directly to a job, manufacturing without utilizing part numbers, and adding to or changing jobs in process.
Progression Series solution	Progression Series solution provides manufacturing, distribution and financial software solutions to medium-sized businesses. The most recent release, Version 7.0, provides a highly flexible and scalable modular, client/server solution used by more than 2,500 businesses and manufacturing customers worldwide.

* The author gratefully acknowledges the research contribution of Sidney Hill, Jr., Marty Weil, and several other original investigators, researchers, authors, and presenters of Manufacturing Systems Special Reports. If this table elucidates the point that the author is making, the credit goes to those original investigators. The author assumes full responsibility for any mistakes and/or omissions.

Table 3.1 Continued

Software Developers	Solver Technologies
R/3	R/3 is the standard in such key industries as oil & gas, chemicals, consumer packaged goods, high technology, and electronics. R/3 helps customers manage comprehensive financial, manufacturing, sales & distribution, and human resources functions.
SyteLine	SyteLine runs ERP, financial administration, advanced planning & scheduling, product configuration, business intelligence, service management, and more. These products are founded on the principle of Customer Synchronized Resource Planning (CSRP), extending ERP beyond the plant walls to integrate manufacturers with their customers, vendors, sales force, distributors, contractors, remote sites, and more.
BPCS Client/Server product line	BPCS delivers agility, re-configurability, and century dating, thereby helping companies achieve significant business benefits by integrating mission-critical operations from global financials to multi-mode manufacturing to total supply-chain management, electronic commerce, and EDI. More than 25,000 sites in various vertical markets—automotive, chemical, consumer goods, electronics, fabrication/assembly, food/beverage, forest products, and pharmaceuticals—have implemented the BPCS ERP system.

Source: Adapted by the author from *Manufacturing Systems 1998 Buyers Guide,* wysiwyg://69/http://www.manufacturingsystems.com/suplment/IBM2.htm.

and addressing networking capabilities. They view Manufacturing Extension Partnership (MEP) as a very important step toward global competitiveness. MEP electronically connects a vast array of technology resources that provide technical assistance with new management and organizational practices, shop floor design, manufacturing process evaluation, workflow education, training programs, and deployment of appropriate advanced manufacturing technologies and manufacturing best practices. To these resources, the larger enterprises are adding services requested by clients, such as user-friendly front-end for transparent access to data repositories resident on the major network systems (e.g., WWW, Gopher, WAIS, etc.).[9] Future programs include additions of databases of best practices, enterprise information, video teleconferencing, online training, product data and electronic commerce capability to the system.

Today's manufacturing enterprises must:

- Transmit data quickly and efficiently from one application to another inside and outside the company's operation.
- Integrate their applications with other companies, suppliers, and customers in a timely and cost-effective manner.
- Connect to directories, design and analysis tools, databases, and search mechanisms for the secure, easy, and timely exchange of manufacturing information in such areas as process analysis, benchmarking, quality assessment, and best practices, as well as connect to a potential user base of 370,000 other small and medium-sized manufacturers.

CommerceNet is an open, Internet-based infrastructure to revolutionize the way companies design, manufacture, sell, and support their products. It makes interactions with customers, suppliers, and partners efficient, high quality, flexible, and responsive.[10] Members of the *CommerceNet* consortium, formed by Smart Valley, Inc., include Hewlett-Packard, Intel, Sun Microsystems, Apple, National Semiconductor, and Texas Instruments.

These advances suggest that today's manufacturing enterprises need technicians and project managers who understand not only ERP solutions through computer technology, but more important, the role of project management in a manufacturing environment. Only then will these project managers:

- Reduce the time to design and manufacture products and get them to market.
- Enhance and adopt key technologies that enable advanced, highly integrated systems to "plug in" a variety of focused engineering tools, thereby ensuring the enterprise the use of additional next generation tools, as well as numerous suppliers.

Modern manufacturing is synonymous with high-technology operations. Therefore, management in manufacturing *is* management of high technology, which requires special attention because high-technology operations have the potential for catastrophe in the event of deliberate or accidental mismanagement. The catastrophe that today's manufacturing enterprises most fear is the loss of competitiveness, which is why enterprises are constantly seeking better and more efficient tools and services to ensure better project management and thereby future competitiveness.

Because project management, as practiced in today's manufacturing enterprises, is so complex, not even the largest software vendors can deliver all the necessary tools and services in one system. Cambridge, Massachusetts-based Forrester Research observes that in an emerging market, production configuration, electronic data interchange, field service modules, and Internet capabilities that extend system access to more users will be the ultimate solution provider in new system construction.

TOWARD THE ULTIMATE FREEWAY

The Internet, in particular, will have an enormous impact on the ability of small and medium-sized manufacturers to engage in effective project management. The two business imperatives of the next millennium are that:

1. Enterprises have end-to-end information within the context of multiple views of the business, rather than just end-to-end integration.
2. All issues are immediate, all business is global, and flexibility is crucial.

The first imperative reflects the reality that companies must rely on a tightly coordinated network of suppliers, subcontractors, customers, and others to maximize their performance in producing and delivering goods and services. This requires managing the complex interrelationships between all trading partners as efficiently as possible. Accomplishing that involves sharing information about every activity involved in getting goods to the customer (including the possible enterprise-wide repercussions of every action) with all members of the project team.

The second imperative is a response to the realization that winning and keeping customers requires not only producing quality goods, but delivering them quickly, regardless of where the customer is located. Accomplishing this requires a common information backbone that links all parts of an enterprise, even within enterprises that conduct business in multiple languages and currencies in many countries. To be effective, the information backbone must encompass state-of-the-art technology, such as the Internet and intranet links that can transcend various languages and currencies, as well as variations in business processes and software applications.

The Internet delivers the technical infrastructure for communicating essential information, including company profiles, directories, e-mail addresses, web links, online schedule and upcoming events information. The collaborative power of this infrastructure adds a planning dimension that is not available through traditional software solutions.[11] Because the Internet is not transaction-oriented but document-centric, it strengthens the documentation process critical to the ongoing vitality of project management.

Many people regard the Internet as an electronic library that allows users to quickly, easily, and accurately search content-rich project information, technical bulletins, and other salient materials. Its rapidly improving secure interface permits project team members to send up-to-the-minute company-sensitive and proprietary information from an underlying data source (e.g., an inventory database) directly to the manufacturers via e-mail, fax, or electronic data interchange. The ability to generate this information dynamically ensures top performance for the project team.

With the inclusion of web browser capabilities, Java, and hypertext markup language (HTML) extensions, the Internet has become very dynamic in helping various project environments become productive.[12] For example, process engineers respond to their on-call support beepers by logging onto the Internet and, using a web browser, they can view the same screen that the operators at the plant are viewing on their consoles. They can use a process recorder (which is similar to a VCR in terms of its capability to rewind and view again) with their web browser and do troubleshooting.

Process analysts can view data from many sources in tabular form, graphical charts, and/or in customized web formats in real time. Web browsers can help users with data sets of graphical animation, alarms, and complex event handling. With such data sets representing the streams of process data, project managers can predict when production, equipment performance, or product quality is deviating from specification, and thereby prevent production of faulty parts. By taking advantage of the capability to detect key trends and spot potential problems before they occur, project managers can achieve faster time-to-market with high-quality products and hence, outpace the competition.

Another facet of the Internet revolution is the "virtual project team" environment. It is now commonplace for manufacturing enterprises to hold conferences in real time, with voice and live console screens simultaneously, with control engineers from corporate and other parts of the global enterprise being linked with local resident manufacturing professionals. The capability to create such virtual project teams and get production, test, manufacturing, monitoring, and control information directly to the best technical and operational personnel, anytime and anywhere, provides an instant advantage to any company.[13] Worldwide manufacturing enterprises are increasingly aware that not just one team develops the best practices. Web conferencing focuses and accelerates the otherwise difficult process of spreading efficient practices throughout the enterprise.

In managing projects, most manufacturing enterprises are making extensive and innovative applications of the Internet to distribute and access, on their own terms, both real-time and historical production data throughout an enterprise. For example, the Measurement Technology Center (MTC) at NASA's Jet Propulsion Laboratory used LabVIEW and Internet technology to monitor experiments of new refrigeration techniques on the space shuttle *Endeavor*. Data were downloaded from *Endeavor* to a LabVIEW program that displayed the data over the web. The results of the experiment can be viewed at www.natinst.com/shuttle.

By facilitating easier access to these data and information, the Internet has become an important internal tracking and archiving tool for production data and text data for engineering groups. Project team members routinely use web pages with interactive links to test program files archived on FTP servers as a primary mechanism for distributing the latest source code versions to team members. Because many organizations within a virtual enterprise share code among different development groups and product teams, using the Internet or intranet as the front end to a central repository is key. Above and beyond yielding the operational and time savings, the Internet is instantly and easily making the process available to the best personnel, thereby ensuring a strategic advantage in the responsiveness and profitability of an enterprise.

The success of the Internet is due to software developers integrating reusable software components and using any language and platform to build web applications. Table 3.2 lists developers actively engaged in the reusable software engineering field.

These software products, applications, and tools adhere to the Internet standards, platform, and languages, and can turn static information into interactive communications that facilitate effective decision making by project managers in manufacturing enterprises.

Project Management: Bringing the Internet to the Factory

As this book goes to press, several manufacturing companies are leveraging the Internet to dramatically improve communications with their partners and customers, especially during the design process.[14] A case in point is Lectra Systems, a worldwide leader in CAD/CAM solutions for the clothing and furniture industries. Lectra has more than 7,000 customers in 80 countries worldwide. Leading manufacturers of leathergoods apparel and upholstery depend on Lectra solutions to execute their work.

Daniel Heran, CEO for Lectra Systems, observes that new communications needs have emerged as a result of the large number of intermediaries spread worldwide. To remain ahead of its competitors, the company realized that it must address its communications needs. Producing ready-to-wear apparel involves various steps, from preliminary design and pattern creation to mass producing the goods. Although the designer may be located in Milan or Paris, the designer's partners may be anywhere in the world. The keys to success are *communication* and *collaboration*.

Table 3.2 New Software for Interactive Communication Over the Internet

Software Developer	Product/Application/Tool Characteristics
Visibility	• Combines information from engineering, inventory control, work-in-process, shop-floor control, and purchasing to plan production
TTW	• For small to medium-sized discrete manufacturers • Focus on scheduling, electronic data interchange, inventory management by location, supplier consignment of inventory, and sales order processing
The Baan Co.	• For automotive, process, electronics, aerospace and defense, and project industries • Year 2000 compliant • Includes web-enabled ERP applications for business-to-business communication within the supply and demand chain • Supports sales forecasting, procurement, inventory, distribution, and transportation applications
Tetra International	• Rough-cut and capacity planning that highlights bottlenecks and resource underutilization and maps production at the shop-floor level • Routing module assists scheduling by machine, work center, or operator • Fully integrated electronic data interchange for customer order management
Systems & Computer Technology (SCT) Corp.	• Electronic data interchange-enabled, object-based system for hybrid process industries • Configures objects and business rules as process work flows to link internal companies, branches, warehouses, and plants with customers, suppliers, and outside suppliers
System Software Assoc. (SSA)	• Configurable order management streamlines order entry • Customer service applications include automatic pricing, inventory allocation, and on-line available-to-promise information • Forecasting can be run independently or with distribution and manufacturing planning functions
Syspro Impact Software	• Manufacturing, financial, and distribution modules integrated to support job-shop, mixed-mode, and repetitive manufacturing environments • Security access definable at group level with ability to view which programs each user is accessing

(continued)

Table 3.2 Continued

Software Developer	Product/Application/Tool Characteristics
Symix Computer Systems	• MRP supports forecasting, master production scheduling, firm planned orders, and order action and exception reports • Supports electronic data interchange (EDI) • Site-level, department-level, and rough-cut capacity planning
SmartShop Software	• Job control feature creates estimates or imports them from estimating systems, enters and reviews orders, processes shipments, and maintains inventory • Customer and vendor tracking also supported • View images, graphs, or multimedia programs of setup procedures
SAP America	• Internet consumer-to-business, business-to-business, and intranet solutions support on-line customer service, checking and replenishing inventories, on-line stock inquiries, order status, internal purchase requistions, and material ordering.
Ross Systems	• Resource capacity planning compares master schedule with critical resource constraints and makes automatic scheduling adjustments • Time-phased material replenishments and transfers to support purchasing, production, and distribution
ROI Systems	• EDI for on-line error reporting, unattended operations, and monitoring incoming and outgoing transactions • Bill of materials, inventory, actual sales demands, forecasting, lead times, and master production schedule used for MRP
Relevant Business Systems	• On-line requirements analysis and action messages ranked by responsibility • Time-sequenced supplies and demands • Plans work orders and purchase requisitions with recommendations for rescheduling according to inventory levels
Qube Connections	• LAN-based ERP software for small to medium-sized manufacturers includes advanced lot and batch tracking, service order tracking, executive information management, and rack position control • View order backlogs, inventory levels, and production trends

(continued)

Table 3.2 Continued

Software Developer	Product/Application/Tool Characteristics
QAD Inc.	• EDI-enabled system collects forecasted demand, inventory, and plant availability to feed a central model that optimizes manufacturing and distribution plans • Decision-support module for follow-up data mining and analysis
ProfitKey International	• Creates orders based on existing requirements or master schedules • Maintains a manufacturing-build schedule or forecast for selected make-to-stock items, manufactured components, or generic items • Levels out workload on an item-by-item basis • Verifies material availability before order release
PowerCerv Corp.	• Graphical client/server ERP system incorporates workflow management and electronic messaging to eliminate nonvalue-added activities • Supports EDI, bar-code data collection, multimedia, and CAD drawing interface
Pivotpoint	• Visibility to plan for multiplant environments • Capacity resource planning features ability to look at best/worst-case scenarios before MRP generation • Optional module for repetitive manufacturers that generates daily schedules and calculates available-to-promise values against a schedule
PeopleSoft	• Production planning uses real-time planning and scheduling engine from Red Pepper Software • Integrates with purchasing and production control • Production control system synchronizes planning and execution • Includes product configurator, cost management, and distribution applications
Oracle Corp.	• Multiplant planning, simulation, and order launching capabilities • Planning encompasses forecast creation, launching production schedules, replenishment orders, and purchase orders • Material schedulers automatically launch and electronically transmit orders directly to suppliers and factories
ONLINE Software Labs	• Focus on planning and execution, utilizing forecasting, real-time inventory management, and distribution requirements planning

(continued)

Table 3.2 Continued

Software Developer	Product/Application/Tool Characteristics
MK Group	• Sites request replenishment through intracompany requests for materials • Features CA-OpenIngres relational data management system for fast processing, data integrity, information access and sharing, data warehousing, and Internet capabilities • Allows for preprogrammed responses to system events • Agent technologies monitor business conditions and send system alerts for critical events
Micro-MRP	• Integrates process and information flow; customer service application supports electronic data interchange and product configuration • Inventory control, sales order entry, lot tracking, and shipping also supported • For make-to-order, make-to-stock, repetitive, and discrete manufacturers
Marcam Systems	• ERP for process manufacturers incorporates production model concepts that allow for custom resource defining • Integrated quality management and activity costing features • Enterprise-wide inventory valuation • Models inputs such as materials, utilities, equipment, facilities, labor, and overhead, and outputs such as finished and recycled products and by-products
MAPICS Inc.	• Finite-capacity planning and scheduling, as well as master production schedule, material requirements, and capacity requirements planning • Electronic commerce supports exchange of data among customers, suppliers, financial institutions, and internal systems • Maintains trading partner relationship definitions, and trading partner interfaces
Made2Manage Systems	• Discrete manufacturers in make-to-order or mixed-mode environments • Workflow management for customer and vendor event notification • Internet capabilities for supplier inventory management and customer inquiries of order status • Product configurator automates custom product activities

(continued)

Table 3.2 Continued

Software Developer	Product/Application/Tool Characteristics
Macola	• Forecasting uses planning bill of materials • Interactive entry of requirement and replenishment orders on master schedule • Merges existing shop orders, purchase orders, and MRP-planned orders • "What-if" analyses and available-to-promise reporting supported • Overscheduled work centers identified through rough cut capacity planning
LK Global Manufacturing	• Make-to-order, batch, and repetitive production flow support • Work-in-process planning with order release, pick list management, shortage control, operation dating, and multilevel trial kitting capabilities • Orders created manually against bar-coded documentation or from MRP module
Lilly Software Assoc.	• Partial or total custom-order manufacturers • Includes support for actual costing, purchasing directly to orders, manufacturing without using part numbers, and changing jobs after they have been released to production • Plans material needs, shop resources, and outside services • Integrated ERP with manufacturing execution and finite scheduling
Jobscope Corp.	• Order-driven manufacturing modes • Integrates estimating, order entry, materials planning, cost control, purchasing, engineering, inventory, and scheduling • EDI-enabled with demand forecasting, multinational, and multicurrency capabilities for worldwide support
JBA International	• Supports full schedule-driven environment and flow line sequencing and control for repetitive manufacturers • Production batch and potent batch balancing for process environments • Mixed-mode capabilities, finite- and infinite-capacity management, and consolidated bill of material for discrete manufacturers
J.D. Edwards	• AS/400-based software with a multimedia environment that emphasizes quick time-to-benefit and high productivity

(continued)

Table 3.2 Continued

Software Developer	Product/Application/Tool Characteristics
	• Coach feature provides ongoing support with voice prompts and multimedia expert for on-line help
	• Automated questionnaire customizes the system
	• Teacher module for multimedia, computer-based training
Intentia North America	• Customer orders generated automatically entered from electronic data interchange (EDI) transactions
	• EDI support for advance customer shipping notice and supplier orders and invoices
	• Procurement initiated by reorder points, MRP, kanban, or directly from customer orders
Infinium Software	• AS/400-based system meets development, production, customer service, financial management, and human resources needs of process manufacturers
	• EDI support for incoming and outgoing orders
	• Monitors loss factors, clingage, and yields
	• Substitutes production items; matches invoices to purchase orders
IMI North America	• Open systems, client/server solution for high-volume consumer and industrial products
	• Unix-based, pull-driven system with electronic messaging architecture that integrates data between customers and suppliers, including orders, order changes and acknowledgments, shipping confirmations, and invoices.
IFS-Industrial & Financial Systems	• Manages several types of manufacturing at one time
	• Production reporting shows all events, enabling comparisons between production times and working hours
	• Long-term, multi-site resources and MRP using internal or external forecasting systems.
ICONtrol	• MRP done in "net change" manner that recalculates only new transactions per item, or "full regeneration," which calculates full demand for a single item
	• Filters planning view by item, warehouse, planner code, or date
GRMS	• EDI support for assemble-to-order, make-to-order, and repetitive environments

(continued)

Table 3.2 Continued

Software Developer	Product/Application/Tool Characteristics
Glovia International	• Open architecture system running on Unix, Novell, and Windows NT platforms • Capacity and MRP • Master production scheduling • Internet/intranet support • Multimedia products • MPS and MRP in real time • Scheduler's Workbench includes on-line analysis and simulation capabilities • Multiple simulations and planning cycles can be stored for comparison • Full lot and serial number traceability
Friedman Corp.	• Inbound/outbound electronic data interchange capabilities, remote order entry, capacity-driven order promising, and product configuration • Inbound/outbound warehouse control, import tracking, and multi-location order sourcing included • Assemble-to-order, make-to-order, configure-to-order, and light engineer-to-order production supported
Fourth Shift Corp.	• On-line manual library from Windows-based CD-ROM help system • Multilevel planning bills of material, lead-time fences, and rough-cut capacity planning capabilities • Manufacturing plan based on master schedule real-time data • Order entry module tracks order backlog, and shipping and invoicing data
FocusSoft	• Client/server system running on Windows NT operating system with Microsoft SQLServer at the back end • Order entry via the Internet, electronic data interchange • Forward and backward scheduling with order prioritization • Capacity planning with "what-if?" scenarios • Notification of past-due resource or late schedules
Expandable Software	• For discrete and batch manufacturers • Repetitive, make-to-order, and mixed-mode production

(continued)

Table 3.2 Continued

Software Developer	Product/Application/Tool Characteristics
	• EDI-enabled, multi-location module inventory control for multiple warehouses
	• Integrates to general ledger for financial applications
Effective Management Systems	• Balances orders against forecast with capacity planning and material requirements planning (MRP) functions
	• Builds long-range MRP plans with continually updated, real-time order entry, purchasing, shipping, and plant-floor information
	• Shop-floor drawings, work instructions, full-motion video, and part programs are supported
Data Works Corp.	• Multiple systems include 32-bit Windows application with graphical user interface
	• Integrated VistaMail e-mail system
	• Security by user ID and menu option
	• On-line edits and/or audits to ensure data integrity
	• Universal database standard for easy import/export
	• Multimedia incorporated with graphics, sound, and full-motion video
Datasul	• Intuitive look and feel
	• Batch or real-time user-definable integration
	• Multiple active cost valuations per product per site
	• Automatic cash flow projection
	• Modular design
	• Multiple currencies and exchange rates supported
	• Summary to detail drill down in modules from a single screen
CMI-Competitive Solutions Inc.	• Passes demand that arrives via electronic data interchange to production scheduling system
	• Level load scheduling analyzes the effect of changing demand on production plans with "what-if?" analyses
	• Supports manual release, backflush by operations, and backflush on receipt material release
Cincom Systems	• For highly engineered products, assemble-to-order, make-to-order, engineer-to-order manufacturers
	• Support for order management, delivery, service, and sales configuration

(continued)

Table 3.2 Continued

Software Developer	Product/Application/Tool Characteristics
Caelus	• Decision-support tools included • Monitoring of business profitability identifies links and trends, analyzes win/loss situations • Just-in-time planning for resources that constrain production and infinite-capacity scheduling for non-bottleneck resources • Work center capacity can be expressed in any unit of measure, with support of overlapping operations and shift-based production • Planning linked with sales order entry to produce delivery dates based on real-time production data
Axis Computer Systems	• Supports metals manufacturers • Multiplant, multinational system integrates with customer-order fulfillment, materials tracking, and load planning and shipping systems • Mixed-mode production, including process and discrete operations
American Software	• For a variety of manufacturing environments, from make-to-order to highly repetitive • MRP II series includes MPS, MRP, Capacity Requirements Planning, Manufacturing Standards, Product Costing, and Shop Floor Control
Alliance Manufacturing Software	• Compares material resources planning schedule with work-center capacity presented in graphical reports • Multilevel security blocks menu items and screens as needed • Easy import and export of data • Supports multiple databases • Multilingual and multicurrency capabilities also are included
Acacia Technologies	• Repetitive manufacturing capabilities include schedule attainment, cycle times, production sequencing, setup/transaction processing, downtime, and on-line quality measurement • Includes order processing, just-in-time deliveries, and EDI capabilities.

Source: Special Reports—Manufacturing Systems, wysiwyg://57/http://www.manufacturingsystems.com/suplment/ERPlist.htm.

A partnership ensued between Lectra and IBM, which brought in Internet connectivity so that Lectra's designers could collaborate on designs and patterns via this medium. A Florentine designer could send a concept to a pattern maker in Barcelona, who could create a model using one of Lectra Systems' solutions. Moreover, by using an Internet browser through IBM's global network, the model could be published on a secured network so that manufacturing facilities in China could set their machines for final production.

Lectra Systems chose to work with IBM because of its ability to offer value-added services with international coverage and its concept approach as a global project management solution. The company's customers are currently exchanging data in their own businesses with all trading partners through a secured internal and external information system. They monitor the design and manufacture of their products in real time, regardless of the time zones in which information technology occurs. The success of this partnership is the result of Lectra aggressively expanding its business by publishing and sharing information, collaborating on projects, and accessing business applications and processes regardless of where employees are located.

CHAPTER 4

Satellite Internet Applications: Project Management Using ICO Global Communications Services

Telephone and the Internet (voice and data) are the two main forms of daily long-distance communications. The Internet even surpasses the telephone, as evidenced by its sudden emergence as a medium capable of serving all communication needs. With the proliferation of satellite launches and vigorous growth of Internet-over-satellite services, most of the material accessed via the Internet might be received by satellite in a few years.*

* This chapter presents some recently conceived satellite-based telecommunications network solutions, in part reflecting the new possibilities of utilizing satellite networks in exchanging large masses of data in record time. The author has not sought to provide a complete presentation of all satellite-based network solutions; rather he has sought to investigate the major ones, as these are being deployed, at a depth sufficient to permit their appraisal. Therefore, any evaluation at this time of these satellite-based telecommunications network solutions, such as Iridium, Globalstar, ICO Global Communications, or Teledesic, can only be rudimentary. Other constellations, such as Ellipso or Orbcomm, which are less developed, are not discussed at all. Since 1998, the satellite-based telecommunications network solution has undergone so many changes, modifications, and failures that the configuration of these networks could be quite different today than might appear in this chapter. Significant help in updating this information through April 1999 was provided by Lloyd Wood of Lloyd's Constellation Group in the UK, and Gary Garriott, Director of Informatics of VITA.

Satellites offer special advantages over landlines for transmitting and receiving large amounts of data. There is no inherent physical limit as to how much bandwidth can be supplied to each customer, because there is no physical link between the satellite and a receiving station on the ground.[1] The only limit to transmission bandwidth is the data capability of the satellite itself, not a physical line that stretches for thousands of kilometers. A connection can be established anywhere within the satellite's broadcast footprint, as long as an antenna on the ground is pointed toward the correct position in the sky. This advantage is creating great interest among global satellite-based telecommunications consortia in the communication needs of isolated rural areas throughout the world.[2]

Similarly, individual users and Internet service providers (ISPs) are showing increased preference for using the Internet-over-satellites because they like what they get: The user makes an "upstream" request, and the response is all unidirectional "downstream" download.

The basic service requirement for mobile users is to be able to access the Internet anywhere, anytime. Satellite networks are now beginning to provide such services by integrating with terrestrial networks. This chapter defines feasible systems for mobile communications based on the integration of the two networks to the largest possible set of common functions at the mobile terminal.

Carrier Networks and Interconnections

The integration between the two networks can be achieved in several different ways, providing different service levels to the user. The following sections identify and differentiate the integration options that are commonly discussed and implemented.

GEOGRAPHICAL INTEGRATION

In this case, the satellite system is complementary to the terrestrial one. The two networks are independently conceived, based on different technologies, and they offer different services to the users. The satellite system's main objective is to offer communications services to areas not served via ground infrastructures, by using either a "terrestrial" or a "satellite" terminal or, as an alternative, *a dual-mode terminal* able to switch between systems. A fixed user originating the call must know the kind of terminal owned by each user receiving the call, to correctly route the call via the terrestrial or the satellite network.

SERVICE INTEGRATION

In the case of service integration, the satellite system parameters are chosen to support services compatible with those provided by the cellular system. Service integration makes it possible for the mobile terminal to access both systems, with appropriate protocol conversions. Service quality is lower than that for geographic integration.

NETWORK INTEGRATION

This type of integration makes service utilization much easier for mobile subscribers. Common network infrastructures allow a fixed user to ask for a connection with a mobile user without having to select the call routing (via terrestrial or satellite network) or knowing which kind of terminal is owned by the mobile user. A unique calling number identifies the generic mobile subscriber, and the network managing units handle the subsequent actions.

SYSTEM INTEGRATION

In this case, handover of calls in progress between terrestrial and satellite cells could be realized each time it becomes necessary for any reason, including partial channel occupancy, degradation of some links, and so on. It must be noted, however, that rerouting procedures are feasible only if the mobile user is equipped with a *dual-mode terminal*.

Satellite Systems

Satellites in Geostationary Orbit (GEO), Low Earth Orbit (LEO), Intermediate Circular Orbit (ICO), Medium Earth Orbit (MEO), and

Highly Elliptical Orbit (HEO) offer different voice, data, and message transmission and reception options.[3] The advantages and disadvantages of these orbital solutions have been discussed in numerous technical and business publications. Based on the performance evaluation and consequent orbital comparison, LEO and ICO solutions are considered appropriate for future mobile communication systems, with L, S, and Ka bands as candidate frequencies (among all the available ones). In particular, only L and S bands are applicable in the case of LEO and ICO systems, with hand-held applications.[4]

In considering the LEO and ICO networks for use in global mobile communications, especially for Internet solutions, it should be noted that the data throughput capacities of LEO telephony systems are not impressive. Teledesic, however, formed in June 1990, is a LEO network in the making which is the satellite equivalent to optical fiber, with broadband channels, low error rates, and low delay.

When Teledesic was first publicized in early 1994, many people found it difficult to comprehend the services that this network would provide. At that time, the Internet was at a relatively primitive stage of development. Shortly thereafter, the world wide web demonstrated the promise of the Internet, with tens of thousands of companies and millions of individuals exploring, publishing, and developing on this new medium. People understood that any and all information could and would be digitized, uploaded, and transmitted anywhere in the world.[5]

By 1995, the world wide web and network-centric computing provided a compelling model for a different kind of telecommunications—switched, broadband services. In my previous book, *Building A Corporate Strategy for Internet Development: The IT Manager's Guide,* published in 1996, I provided authoritative studies indicating how peer-to-peer networking was transforming the way individuals live and businesses create value, based on the ubiquity and exponential improvements of personal computing. This trend made the Teledesic concept a digital revolution, with its switched connections to communicate from anyone to anyone, and broadband to allow the transmission of all forms of digital information—voice, data, videoconferencing, and interactive multimedia.

The Teledesic satellite network configuration, and the number of satellites to be included in the constellation, have been modified in recent years. The current design brings wireless access to advanced network connections. To obtain the bandwidth required for fiberlike service, Teledesic must operate its network in the 20 to 30 GHz range (Ka band). Sending signals in those frequencies is problematic because of rain attenuation and blockage by terrain, foliage, and buildings. To overcome these problems, the Ka band must have a line of sight from the user terminal to the satellite, which makes it more appropriate for fixed applications, or mobile applications like maritime and aviation use, where line of sight is not an issue.

The Teledesic network is a good choice for broadband services to accommodate sophisticated real-time applications, such as world wide web, if the intent is to support a fixed application.[6] The capability of accessing much of the same information on a web page via e-mail is increasing, as is the possibility of providing such services through small communications satellites in low-earth orbit (LEO) with corresponding low-cost, ground-based hardware. There is a resurgence of interest in narrowband, as end-users learn that e-mail can provide many types of data and information that broadband is supposed to provide.[7]

The Problem

Forty-nine of the world's poorest countries are characterized with teledensities of fewer than one (0.72) telephone per 100 residents. People living in these countries are effectively shut out of the Internet revolution. Although the International Telecommunications Union (ITU) predicts average growth in 54 of the poorest countries to 2.17 telephones per 100 residents by the year 2000, rural areas are likely to continue to suffer because privatization is unlikely to produce any significant changes for these areas. Most urban-oriented enterprises have no profit-borne incentive to improve and expand service in rural areas with sparse populations and dispersed markets. Another facet of privatization, at least in some Latin American and African countries, is that Internet services tend to be provided through the newly privatized companies in a monopolistic fashion. Belize, for example, does not permit commercial electronic mail service by third-party resellers of local and international telephone circuits.

Economic and regulatory hurdles are reasons for a general lack of confidence that priority will ever be given to most rural and isolated areas. Based on this, one must also understand that crucial data and information are needed at a specific time for any project implementation in a rural environment: If delivered late, data and information may lose their value. Even more important are human and material resources that may be wasted if not used when critically needed.

Planners often view projects as objectives compartmentalized into specific activities with discrete beginning and ending points. However, field staff considers accomplished objectives as having successfully recognized and exploited windows of opportunity. When the window is open, it is critical to have the correct information available at that time. When the window is closed (e.g., field staff promised skeptical village leaders information on a new agricultural, environmental, or medical project, but could not deliver) it may be difficult if not impossible to reactivate interest. Village leaders, with numerous other demands made on their time, move on to other projects.

Conversely, when information-communication channels are reliable, interesting and unexpected things can happen. A case in point is VITA's (Volunteers in Technical Assistance) experience in the use of LEO satellites to provide near real-time services. VITA supports a ground station in Tanzania, which provides connection to a LEO satellite. The ground station has used VITA's existing Internet gateway to order parts and retrieve technical information for the construction of two small aircraft built from kits. One such aircraft is already flying and meeting various needs in remote regions of that country. This use was not predicted when the ground station was first established.[8]

To underscore the basic point, information and data retrieval capability enhances project planning and implementation in isolated rural areas. Only through query-response can one obtain the most up-to-date technical information that meets the needs of scientific, engineering, or other development projects. Each response provides more feedback with which the query could be further refined. This suggests that a good network service is one that: (1) reduces the turnaround time, and (2) installs reliable communication modes that can ensure speed from isolated areas for any number of rural projects and activities. Indeed, all project planners experienced in international developments concur that the availability of such capabilities will greatly benefit any project development activity. To them, instant access is not mandatory; but if the turnaround is measured in hours (or a couple of days) as opposed to weeks or months, their efficiency would increase tenfold, dramatically impacting the functions and activities they are performing in a particular isolated or rural environment.[9]

The State of Network Services in Africa

In Africa, the cost of the various modes of telecommunication is prohibitively high. For example, it takes 10 minutes to read 2,000 words aloud, and a 10-minute voice phone call from the Netherlands to Ghana costs 34 US Dollars. The fax machine may be faster and cheaper (2,000 words in a compact font will take two minutes to send), but fax transmission costs 7 US Dollars. By contrast, an e-mail message of 2,000 words (about 12 kilobytes or 96 kilobits in digital terms), sent via a modem with a throughput speed of 14 kilobits per second, will take seven seconds to reach Accra from Amsterdam and cost 0.40 US Dollar. Furthermore, if the telephone line is good, a 28 kilobits per second modem working at full speed will further halve the transmission charge—making it 175 times cheaper than a voice phone call across the same distance. This makes it abundantly clear that e-mail is not a luxury but a necessity in the developing world—particularly in Africa. In a continent where the postal services will often deliver only to post office boxes, a large number of connections to the Internet would be very useful. E-mail service is the only mode of international telecommunication that Africa can quickly install and easily afford.[10] The only African countries currently connected to the Internet with international links faster than 64 Kbps are South Africa, Egypt, Kenya, and Tunisia.[11] (Refer to Figure 4.1.)

Table 4.1 shows that there are several African countries with existing or planned BitNet, FidoNet, and UUCP services which provide lim-

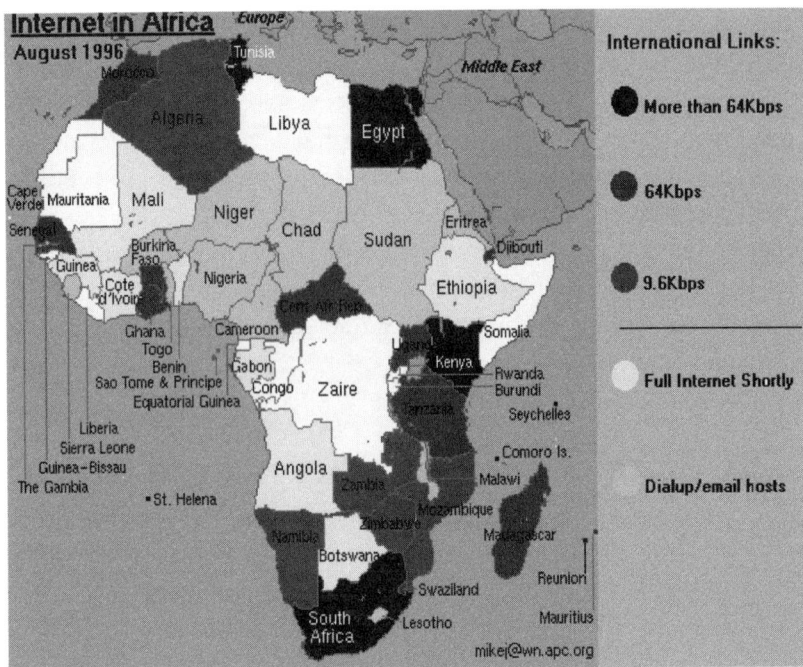

Figure 4.1 Internet in Africa

Source: Jensen, Mike, *Bridging the Gaps in Internet Development in Africa*, IDRC Study, August 31, 1996, http://www.idrc.ca/acacia/studies/ir-gaps5.htm

ited access to the Internet. The existing projects involve only UUCP/FidoNet networks, whereas the newer projects aim at expanding Internet services.[12]

Table 4.2 shows that electronic mail and News are the only services offered by all the networks available in Africa, including the Internet. BitNet offers a utility that is similar to Internet FTP, through its file servers. BitNet and FidoNet do not permit remote log-in, thereby making interactiveness impossible. Services such as Gopher, WAIS, FTP, or WWW are, therefore, not available.[13] This environment justifies the need to investigate how to improve the basic e-mail service to make it more relevant and meaningful for the particular data and information needs of the project planners and their field support personnel.

Table 4.1 State of Network Services in Africa

Existing Networks	Type	Services
BitNet (only Egypt and Tunisia are connected)	A network of computers linked point to point by exclusive connections, with each of the computers (a node) maintaining a unique name. Connected to other networks including the Internet. Interconnection permits the exchange of messages between the two networks.	The users' addresses are presented in the same manner as in the Internet (i.e., user@mode). Offers three basic communications tools: Messages File transmission Electronic mail Services rendered through servers, which • respond to requests received via messages or electronic mail • may be accessed through the Internet Types: File servers Users' address servers List servers Relay Type servers
FidoNet (countries with some sites connected: Algeria, Angola, Botswana, Ethiopia, Gambia, Ivory Coast, Kenya, Lesotho, Malawi, Mauritius, Mozambique, Nigeria, Senegal, South Africa, Tunisia, Tanzania, Uganda, Zambia, and Zimbabwe).	Uses the telephone network as a means of communication between computers equipped with a modem. Transmission of data is organized to limit the costs of communication.	Electronic mail and News at low cost between BBS (electronic billboards). Connected to the Internet and UUCP. The Internet handles traffic to certain destinations, especially between Europe and the United States, thereby limiting costs.

(continued)

Table 4.1 Continued

Existing Networks	Type	Services
UUCP (Unix to Unix Copy) Networks (There are several individual UUCP networks which have merged into a large network known as UUCP. Has more than one million users).	Collection of protocols developed to copy files between Unix systems using telephone lines and modems. Networks of computers that exchange electronic mail and sometimes News. Distinguish themselves from other networks by their lack of centralization.	Provide indirect Internet access by tapping in-coming information via a computer connected to the Internet. The Intertropical Network of Computers (French acronym: RIO) • a UUCP network established by the French overseas agency ORSTOM; • provides Internet access only for electronic mail in: Burkina Faso, Cameroon, Congo, Ivory Coast, Madagascar, Mali, Mauritius, Niger, Senegal, and Togo. In southern Africa, UUCP links exist between the Internet in South Africa and Lesotho, Mozambique, Swaziland, and Zimbabwe.

Other Network Projects

Global Networking Workshop enumerated the following projects:

NGONET	Provides electronic mail access throughout the African continent via FidoNet.	Almost complete.
ESANET (Eastern Southern African NETwork)		Links researchers in eastern and southern Africa by electronic mail Associated with the NGONET.
HealthNet created by SatelLife, an American NGO PADISNET (Pan African Documentation Centre Network)	A satellite network for exchange of medical information at low cost	

(continued)

Table 4.1 Continued

Other Network Projects		
WEDNET	A network for data and information exchange.	Links researchers working on women's projects for the management of natural resources in Senegal, Ghana, Burkina Faso, Nigeria, Sudan, Kenya, Zimbabwe, Zambia, and Canada.
MANGO	Electronic billboard in Zimbabwe.	
ARSONET		Links centers located in Ethiopia, Senegal, Kenya, and Egypt via the FidoNet.

Source: Compiled by author from various sources.

Store-and-forward e-mail is currently operational in dozens of African countries. One LEO communications satellite which has been available for well over a decade is the isolated store-and-forward satellite, which follows an inclined or a polar orbit at an altitude of about 700 kilometers. This kind of satellite takes one to two hours to circle the planet, which turns on its axis at the same time. As a result, every place on earth is covered by the footprint at least four times a day for about 15 minutes. This is the window of opportunity to exchange e-mail between the satellite and a user on the ground. When the satellite appears above the horizon, all e-mail is automatically sent upward; the satellite stores it, and then drops it as soon as a preassigned Internet host equipped with a transceiver (transmitter/receiver) comes in sight. From the host, the

Table 4.2 Comparison of Services Offered by Different Types of Networks

	E-mail	NEWS	FTP	Telnet	Gopher	WAIS	WWW
Internet	X	X	X	X	X	X	X
BitNet	X	X	X				
FidoNet	X	X					
UUCP	X	X					

message is forwarded via the Internet to the appropriate person anywhere on earth, who can then send a reply just as easily.

VITA's proposed communication system is a good example of the use of store-and-forward mode.[14] The essential elements of the system are the VITASAT-1R (FAISAT-2v) satellite and User Terminal (UTs, computers, and software) attached to Messaging Terminals (MTs). These send and receive messages from the satellite as short data packets or large files. MTs communicate with the satellite at either 2400 bps or 9600 bps.

Typically, the MT receives a message from one or more UTs and sends this message to the satellite, which, in turn routes it to a satellite gateway in Capetown, South Africa, or Andenes, Norway. The satellite gateway makes the routing decisions to deliver the message to a local UT or to send it through the corresponding Internet gateway. If, however, the destination is a remote UT, the satellite gateway sends it back to the satellite and from there it is routed to the proper MT

Two other elements, the Master Ground Station (MGS) and the Network Control Center (NCC), should also be noted. MGS controls the operation of the satellite constellation, whereas the NCC is assigned the tasks of handling the data flow and controlling the Internet gateways. Figure 4.2 illustrates the network. The satellite's mass storage processor stores the e-mail packets until the satellite passes over a Satellite/Internet gateway station. As the satellite appears over the horizon, the station:

1. Requests and communicates over a dedicated downlink channel, while MT traffic to the satellite continues

2. Commands the mass storage processor to downlink the messages it has collected

3. Uplinks at 19.2 kpbs any messages to remote users that have arrived at the gateway in time for that satellite pass

This remarkably efficient and inexpensive way to exchange e-mail with anyone, anywhere on earth deserves much more attention than it actually gets. The problem is that there are two limitations of the store-and-forward e-mail. First, the service is not continuous—the user must wait for the satellite to pass above a particular location for uploading and downloading. Second, the service does not address the mobile user's

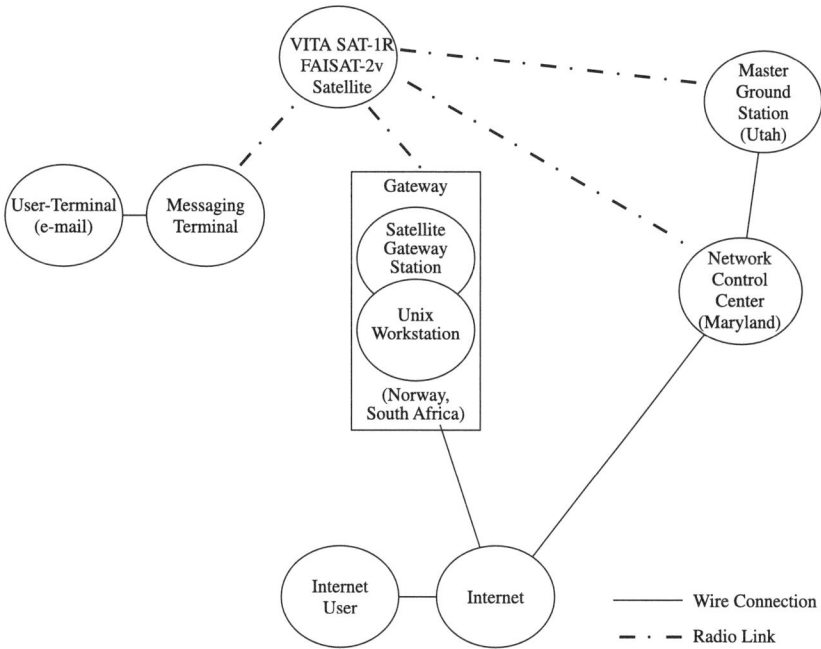

Figure 4.2 VITA Proposed Communication System

Source: Gary L. Garriott, *Low Earth Orbiting Satellites and Internet-Based Messaging Services*, Volunteers in Technical Assistance, http://www.iif.hu/inet_96/g1/g1_1.htm

needs, particularly those who are implementing priority projects in remote areas of the world. Only fixed locations are able to benefit from the store-and-forward e-mail service.

In order for e-mail and the Internet to be successful in Africa, the continent will need solid, large-scale, affordable international connections with the rest of the world. That justifies the introduction of worldwide "mobile phone" systems by Iridium, Globalstar, and ICO.[15] All of them will be in place for a wireless communications system within three to four years, notwithstanding Iridium and Globalstar's recent failures in orbit or during launch.

Table 4.3 compares the services and cost of the major operators, including Teledesic. Table 4.4 provides information on their Orbits and Geometry, whereas Table 4.5 summarizes the frequencies and miscellaneous other information on the four operators.[16]

Table 4.3 Services and Cost

Services and Cost	ICO	Globalstar	Iridium	Teledegic
Service types	voice, data, fax, short	voice, data, fax, paging,	voice, data, fax, paging,	voice, data, video, multimedia, collaborative computing
	messaging service	short message service, position location	messaging, position location	
Voice (kbps)	4.8	adaptive 2.4/4.8/9.6	2.4	
Data (kbps)	2.4/9.6	7.2 sustained throughput	Not offered	16–2048 (voice & data). Higher rates to some larger terminals.
Voice circuits/ satellite	4500	Not available	1100 (power limited) 3840 (max available)	More than 600,000 16 kbps channels
Dual-mode Mobile Terminals?	yes	yes	yes	N/A
Hand-held Mobile Terminals?	yes	yes	yes	Fixed only
System cost (million US$)	2600	3.3B	3700	9000
Mobile Terminal cost (US$)	"several hundred"	750	2500–3000	—
Satellite lifetime (years)	10	7.5	5	10
Call rates (US$/minute) (see note)	1–2	0.35–0.53 wholesale	3	—
FCC licensed?	no	yes	yes	yes
Operation scheduled (year)	2000	1999	1999	2003

Source: Adapted from The Big LEO Tables by Lloyd Wood (L.Wood@Surrey.ac.uk), with additional updated information from the respective company brochures.

Caution: The system cost figures contain different elements that may not be strictly comparable. For instance, the figures may include only initial capital cost, which would make a significant difference when comparing the cost of the short-lived LEO systems (5 to 7.5 years) to the longer-lived MEO systems (10 to 15 years.)

Note also that the call rates may involve different elements; for example, Globalstar's rates do not include the additional cost the service providers will have to add to recover the cost of a Globalstar earth station gateway.

Table 4.4 Orbits and Geometry

Orbits and Geometry	ICO	Globalstar	Iridium	Teledesic
Orbit class	MEO	LEO	LEO	LEO
Altitude (km)	10355	1410	780	1375
Number of satellites	10 active 2 in-orbit spares	48 active 8 in-orbit spares	66 active 6 in-orbit spares	288+ active spares
Number of planes	2	8	6	12
Inclination	45	52	86.4	84.7
Period (minutes)	358.9	114	100.1	113.2
Satellite visibility time (minutes)	115.6	16.4	11.1	4.7
Minimum mobile terminal elevation angle	10	10	8.2	40
Minimum mobile link one-way propagation delay (ms)	34.5	4.63	2.60	4.5
Maximum mobile link one-way propagation delay (ms)	48.0	11.5	8.22	6.5
Minimum Earth Station elevation angle	—	10	8.5	—
Number of Earth Stations	12	< 100	15–20 planned; 11 constructed	—
Coverage	global	within ± 70° latitude	global	global

Source: Adapted from The Big LEO Tables by Lloyd Wood (L.Wood@surrey.ac.uk), with additional updated information from the respective company brochures.

Differentiation

Iridium aims at the high-end travelers' market, whereas Globalstar targets the complementary market near the big cities. Globalstar foresees that 90 percent of the entire market will be in the vicinity of such big centers. Teledesic's LEO proposal, as discussed earlier, is the first broadband LEO. However, there are major concerns about all these systems.

Table 4.5 Frequencies and Miscellaneous Information

Frequencies and miscellaneous information	ICO	Globalstar	Iridium	Teledesic
Mobile downlink frequencies (MHz)	1980–2010 (S-band)	2483.5–2500.0	1616.0–1626.5 (L-band)	Ka-band
Mobile uplink frequencies (MHz)	2170–2200	1610.0–1626.5 (L-band)	1616.0–1626.5 (L-band)	Ka-band
Feeder uplink frequencies (GHz)	5 (C-band)	5.091–5.250 (C-band)	27.5–30.0 (Ka-band)	Ka-band
Feeder downlink frequencies (GHz)	7 (C-band)	6.875–7.055 (C-band)	18.8–20.2 (Ka-band)	Ka-band
Handover performed?	yes	yes, seamless	yes	yes

L-band is 0.5 to 1.5GHz; C-band is 4 to 8 GHz; Ku-band is 10.9 to 17 GHz; and Ka-band is 18 to 31 GHz. The band names originate from the names of the original waveguide sizes chosen in the 1940s—Ku is under K-band, whereas Ka is above K-band.

Source: Adapted from The Big LEO Tables by Lloyd Wood (L.Wood@surrey.ac.uk), with additional updates from the respective company brochures.

The choice of orbital configuration must take into account the feasibility and technical risk of the satellites, as well as the quality of service to be delivered to the user. As it stands today, Teledesic's network will have 288 satellites in orbit, which portend problems for procuring and managing the required number of satellites, given Globalstar and Iridium's recent satellite losses at launch and in orbit.

Technology studies of the LEO, MEO, and GEO satellite constellations concluded that MEO represents a reasonable implementation and schedule. A higher satellite orbit means less likelihood of signal blockage and fewer call handoffs, thereby ensuring superior quality of service.[17] The first column of Table 4.4 indicates that among the four services reviewed, only ICO Global Communications is utilizing the MEO orbital configuration to offer best overall service quality for the desired market from the year 2000.[18]

ICO's Market Strategy

The commercial strategy of ICO has remained consistent since its establishment. ICO offers real-time mobile voice communication systems from hand-held telephones useful for travelers in isolated areas. ICO also plans to complement its core product—hand-held dual-mode global phone service (refer to Table 4.3), with additional offerings such as data communications for remote communities, and specialty applications. Olof Lundberg, CEO of ICO Global Communications, observes that these applications challenge the traditional image of the portable phone as simply a useful accessory and give the portable phone a far broader reach. Lundberg sees ICO's role as that of providing a global infrastructure that can be used for many different types of communication.[19]

Both individual users and the Internet service providers are excited about the use of satellites with the Internet. The uses are limited only by the creativity of the operator. Test marketing has identified key applications for wireless e-mail service in these markets:[20]

- Transportation
- Automotive
- Environmental
- Health
- Education
- Retail
- Business
- Government
- Consumers

ICO dual-mode phones, in addition to voice communication, can support e-mail with slow data links to the Internet—a 2,400 bit-per-second uplink and a 9,600 bit-per-second downlink. This would require a robust hand-held e-mail terminal with alphanumeric keypad and a display for the entry and a display of text messages of variable lengths.

Notwithstanding the slow data throughput capacity, Internet e-mail traffic via the ICO system comprising the space segment and ICONET, the company's dedicated ground network,[21] facilitates project management in various markets.

Table 4.6 shows that ICO's primary marketing strategy is to tap uncovered cellular customers. Its initial research has identified several potential target markets.[22]

The company's services are designed to be fully integrated with existing and future cellular and personal communication services. This will enable ICO to access potential subscribers through existing cellular and PCS distribution channels. These potential subscribers are:

- Existing cellular users who want service in areas covered by incompatible systems or not covered by any terrestrial means
- Mobile communications users located in areas with no form of terrestrial coverage
- Aeronautical, maritime, and long-distance land transport operators
- People living in rural and remote areas lacking adequate telecommunications infrastructure

Among these potential subscribers are mobile businesspeople who are very interested in data over the ICO system. Their numbers are ever increasing, which means the number of potential e-mail, Internet, and world wide web users is also increasing.

Mobile Internet e-mail applications will empower project managers and their field support personnel working in isolated and rural areas of Africa, and other areas of the world where no other means of communication exist, to exchange information with remote databases.[23] E-mail, as discussed in more detail in Accessing The Internet By E-mail (Doctor Bob's guide to Offline Internet Access, mail-server@rtfm.mit.edu), is capable of recalling and using some of the tools "hidden" by the ease of web access.

Table 4.6 ICO's Market Strategy/Projected Market Share

Market Strategy	Projected Market Share (percentages)
Cellular customers	42 percent
Trucking	28 percent
International travel	15 percent
Rural areas	10 percent
Aeronautical telephone	4 percent
Maritime	1 percent

Source: ICO Global Communications.

A Model for the Establishment of a Mobile Internet Infrastructure within the African Context

Developing information services with users is an uncommon strategy among satellite-based telecommunications consortia. To meet the needs of local communities and match their ability to pay, ICO is setting up a number of companies with links to established firms in specific regions. Mechanisms for providing training and continuous support, delivered for and by the organizations and users involved, are an important part of this approach. Pat McDougal, Senior Vice President, Strategic Business Development, is responsible for building ICO's global commercial relationships. His division is forging agreements with various public and private organizations that currently manage the telecoms environment in every country in the world.[24]

This business development effort by ICO provides an interesting case study of Internet issues in the African context, both from a technical and economic environment perspective. A number of privately held Internet Service Providers have moved into commercial operation using links to South Africa and the United Kingdom. The prospect of private organizations carrying telecommunications traffic threatens the franchises of the PTTs. Further, the rapidly increasing demands from the customer base have placed the PTTs in a difficult position of having to deliver services they are ill-equipped to provide. ICO's challenge is to develop a business plan for the PTTs in Africa, which would allow them to deploy the Internet in an aggressive and proactive fashion, while limiting their risks and optimizing the utility of the private investment capital available in the market. The model that ICO chooses to implement must place the PTTs as national backbone providers.

ICO's major strategic investors are telecoms services companies that already have strong existing customer bases. One of the company's largest African investors, Telkom South Africa, plans to use the ICO system to provide a nationwide phone service. Other African investors are Liberia's Bureau of Maritime Affairs, Satfone Maroc of Morocco, Mauritius Telecom, Kenya Post & Telecommunications, Intelcam of

Cameroon, Sonatel of Senegal, Nitel of Nigeria, and Arento of Egypt. Inmarsat shareholding means that five other African nations—Algeria, Gabon, Ghana, Mozambique, and Tunisia—also have a strong interest in ICO.

The PTTs, in concert with other service providers/dealers, are responsible for service delivery to the customer. ICO plans to operate through strong local distribution partners, which include the PTTs and other operators, distributors, service providers, and dealers. As Figure 4.3 indicates, ICO wants to leverage its partners' existing distribution channels to market products and services. Many of these locally established partners will provide locally relevant information analysis and dissemination, as well as access to Internet telecommunication services such as electronic mail. Mobile access to Internet telecommunication services can, indeed, emerge as an ICO special service in its own right in Africa, as basic electronic mail services replace telephone and fax services as a very low-cost medium for sending messages between individuals and organizations responsible for project planning and implementation.

The implementation of the model in Africa brings to the fore a series of issues specific to the African context and in turn the appropriateness of the mobile Internet model. The most basic issue is the reliability and availability of the access and transmission networks. Wireless data access becomes a critical factor in making Internet e-mail services available. Perhaps the most pressing issue is how Internet can provide direct benefit to the mobile customer base of a developing nation.[25] Within this context, the ability to integrate Internet e-mail into existing communications activities and applications is crucial.

In the preceding sections, we discussed limitations to growth, including:

- Lack of any national access network.
- Lack of domestic transmission infrastructure.
- Limited economic rationale for connecting rural and isolated areas, and other factors.

In this type of environment, the following could serve as possible accelerators of growth:[26]

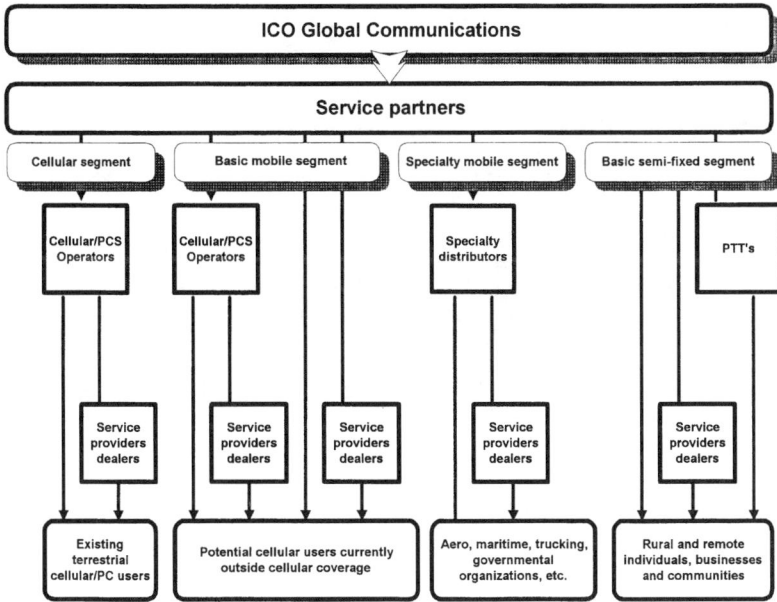

Figure 4.3 ICO's Service Partners

Source: ICO Global Communications, Inc.

- National Access facilities will significantly increase the growth of the Internet market as they make connectivity accessible to rural users and free significant resources at a service provider, dealer/distributor level to compete on other value-adding activities, thereby increasing the local benefits of connecting.
- Aggressive telecoms expansion in making more lines available for access will provide momentum.
- Increased availability of application services, such as mobile e-mail, will accelerate growth of the market.

The Market Model

The market model for Africa places ICO in the significant role of providing the long-haul capacity for all mobile traffic within Africa, and managing all international Internet traffic through its satellite connectivity. As illustrated in Figure 4.4, the ICO system integrates mobile satellite communications capability with terrestrial networks (PSTN, PLMN, and PSPDN) and offers services similar to normal cellular phones in outdoor environments through dual-mode hand-held mobile telephones. It can route calls from terrestrial networks through ground stations, called Satellite Access Nodes or "SANs," which select a satellite through which the calls will be connected. The benefit of this configuration is that it places the PTTs and the other partners in a dominant position in the local market, while they leverage the ICO transmission core competence to offer value-added Internet services.

PTTs will offer:

- *National access* for use by individual customers
- *International backbone* for the creation of Internet service hubs serving medium-sized businesses.

The individual and mobile users may be physically linked into ICONET—the ICO's infrastructure—but the services will be sold by the PTTs and other service partners. More specifically, the following service roles of ICO, PTTs, and other service providers will emerge:

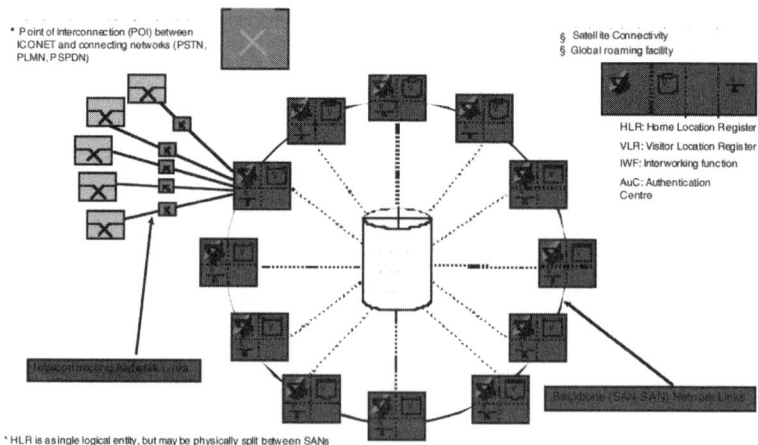

Figure 4.4 ICONET and Its Interconnections

Source: ICO Global Communications, Inc.

ROLE OF ICO

- International access through interconnection between ICONET and PSTN, PLMN, and PSPDN.

ROLE OF PTTs

- The PTT remains the sole supplier of the local backbone and the international Internet link.
- The PTT provides technical support to the end users.
- The PTT maintains service levels by expanding the network's capacity based on increases in demand.

ROLE OF OTHER SERVICE PROVIDERS

- The other service providers will compete on quality and value-added services at the customer interface.
- The other service providers will support the users with specific user requirements, which might include installation of equipment and training.

While setting up satellite-based Internet services in Africa, the author dealt with local entrepreneurs and small and medium-sized enterprises throughout Africa. His experiences indicate that the requests for providing e-mail services are accelerating. Existing service providers, dealers, and distributors need packages of incentives to enable them to take the risks involved in providing rural and remote Internet services. To that end, ICO's business agreements with the local service providers and the regulatory authorities will be the most important instruments. These are the entities with which ICO must organize interconnection of its network and arrange distribution and local deals. Incentives could be spelled out in terms of arranging technology transfer, offset coproduction, and codevelopment for manufacturing the handsets or other terminal equipment, and establishing training schemes. To date, ICO has signed distribution agreements in several countries.[27] The agreements allocate the service distribution rights for specific countries or regional markets to ICO's service partners or to joint ventures established to provide service distribution. The agreements suggest that ICO's strength lies in its business approach and its commitment to serving early and future data markets.

Because ICO may be vying for an unestablished market demand, it must work with local communities to ensure that its services match people's requirements. The first requirement, which underlies and shapes the rest, is that ICO's business agreements must be comprehensive. The author's experience in establishing international sales and distribution networks in Africa is that the local entrepreneurs want the deals to be specific in terms of:

- The objectives of the parties
- Form of equity
- Tax structuring
- Investment contributions
- Business plan and financing
- Future access to capital
- Management, particularly voting control
- Intellectual property rights and technology transfer

Careful treatment of these points will draw out the alliance partner commitments. Appendix C puts these joint venture plans and actions in perspective.

Second, in Africa, the Internet is being introduced for the most part as a business. Several projects are underway.[28] Descriptions of these projects follow.

UNEPnet and Mercure

Mercure is a suite of 16 earth stations providing global telecommunications via the Intelsat system. Much of the data that measure status and change in the environment are being gathered by automated systems (such as satellites) and being fed electronically into various networks. The ability to use these data to make informed decisions about sustainable environmental management depends on the ability to locate, combine, compare, and collate data and on collaboration and communication between the data gatherers and data users. UNEPnet and Mercure will provide the means for UNEP's constituents to participate in and benefit from these processes.

The Leland Initiative

The project emphasizes a public/private partnership approach both in Africa and the United States to bring full Internet connectivity to as many as 20 countries in sub-Saharan Africa served by USAID. USAID will achieve Leland Initiative goals by creating a sustainable Internet service provider industry and enhancing user applications for sustainable development.

AfricaLink

AfricaLink is a project that targets the end users of information technologies, particularly scientists and policy makers who are members of USAID partner networks in agricultural, environmental, and natural resource management sectors. Within the context of each country's existing infrastructural and regulatory environment, AfricaLink works with network leadership to implement simple strategies for Internet access, especially access to electronic mail.

SatelLife/HealthNet

HealthNet is an information service, operated by SatelLife, that connects health care workers around the world. HealthNet uses the most affordable and appropriate technology to offer electronic mail and conferences as well as access to several electronic journals and publications. It also provides access to databases and experts. For its Internet users, HealthNet offers pointers to useful health mailing lists, world wide web home pages, Gopher, and FTP sites on the Internet. HealthNet, licensed by VITA,[29] is currently operational in the following African countries: Botswana, Burkina Faso, Cameroon, Eritrea, Ethiopia, Gambia, Ghana, Kenya, Malawi, Mali, Mozambique, South Africa, Sudan, Tanzania, Uganda, and Zimbabwe.

The Internet Society (ISOC)

The ISOC plays an active role in training African systems operators from countries that are either not yet connected to the Internet or are developing and enhancing an initial national Internet. Among the organization's goals are:

- Training a critical mass of trainer/professionals in network infrastructure, transport, services, and management to support an extension of meaningful Internet-related activities within the countries represented;
- Identifying and sharing individual and institutional contacts, as well as information sources that will assist the process of national development, using international Internet connections;
- Increasing the level of cooperation among existing projects and activities for establishing data networks in developing countries.

Africa Conference on Telecommunications, Broadcasting, and Informatics

This is an annual conference that provides an opportunity for African ministers and high-level public and private sector delegates (such as heads of African PTOs) to meet with ranking government officials and business executives from the United States and Europe. Conference participants have traditionally used the venue to discuss partnerships and joint ventures aimed at developing telecommunications, broadcasting, and electronic networking in Africa. At the most recent AFCOM meeting, participants discussed policy issues, financing, cellular developments, satellite technology, future joint ventures, and a host of other topics related to the development of telecommunications, broadcasting, and informatics in Africa.

AT&T's Africa ONE Project

The network is supported by both the Regional African Satellite Communications Organization (RASCOM) and the Pan-African Telecommunications Union (PATU).

Indigenous Private Ventures

Many of these local companies also supply goods and services to the multinational companies, NGOs, and donor agencies within their countries.

Nii Quaynor is a Ghana businessman who set up that country's first Internet service provider. Like many other entrepreneurs, he set up the Internet node himself. There are several case studies in *Bridge Builders*, written by Moussa Fall in Senegal, Charles Musisi in Uganda, and Neil Robinson in Zambia, that demonstrate entrepreneurial spirit in Africa. Refer to *Bridge Builders: African Experiences with Information and Communication Technology* (1996), Panel on Planning for Scientific and Technological Information (STI) Systems in Sub-Saharan Africa, National Research.

Other Initiatives

ORSTOM, the French research agency, is active in establishing African networking connectivity through its RIO network. Rionet is an international electronic network that links 25 Unix hosts in 10 countries, with approximately 80 access points (standard terminals or local nodes). In sub-Saharan Africa, Rionet provides e-mail connectivity from Burkina Faso, Cameroon, Cote d'Ivoire, Madagascar, Mali, Mauritius, Niger, Senegal, and Togo. It offers e-mail, file transfer, mailing lists, and user directory. It also provides all users a gateway to the French Minitel network.

The government of the Netherlands is very interested in helping to develop high-bandwidth Internet connections to universities in eight African countries and the Association of African Universities. It is also in the process of establishing an African Communications Institute that will focus on many of these issues.

The above are just some of the current Internet network development initiatives in Africa.[30] As ICO endeavors to profile the company as the one that meets local needs, it must develop working relationships with these international, governmental, and private groups. Kahya Dlukulu, ICO's regional general manager for Africa, points out that the company is engaged in regular discussions with regional economic groupings, including Economic Commission of West African States

(ECOWAS) and Union des Etats de l'Afrique Centrale (UDEAC), to develop trans-border agreements and to ensure that the expected growth in telecoms services is in sync with regional development strategies.[31] Such activities should go a long way toward establishing ICO technical and commercial excellence. In its third year of implementation, ICO is prepared to launch a full commercial service. This case study underscores that now is the best time to introduce mobile Internet e-mail as a service and that it is advantageous for ICO to include mobile Internet e-mail solution in its service portfolio.

CHAPTER 5

Internet Caching

Caching Considerations

Since 1997, the world wide web has simplified the way users explore and retrieve networked information. Consequently, the web has made a major impact on networked information systems and on the underlying resource of network bandwidth. Figure 5.1 illustrates how the structure of the Internet requires an increasingly large pipe to go deeper into the core of the network.* Bandwidth costs and the demand for data grow exponentially as distance increases. In the beginning, those costs were borne by the public infrastructure and subsidies that founded the Internet. However, commercialization has exhausted the capacities of the original Internet. Without any action, the network will become clogged and the origin servers will be unable to sustain the high load. Because both effects will increase latency, people throughout the world will experience long waiting times to get the requested objects from the Internet.

This situation requires an investigation of the model of a caching solution. Caching addresses the redundant movement of static informa-

---

* This chapter draws heavily upon the works of Robert E. Lee, Andre de Jong, Ton Verschuren, Henry Bekker, Ingrid Melve, Jon Knight, Martin Hamilton, Margaret Dumont, and Michael Sparks. The author gratefully acknowledges the intellectual contribution of these original investigators, researchers, authors, and presenters. If the tables, charts, and other materials explain the underlying concepts successfully, the credit goes to those original thinkers. However, the author of this chapter is solely responsible for any mistakes and/or omissions.

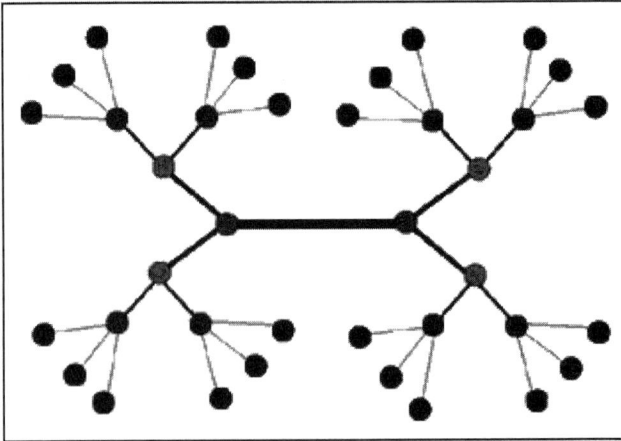

Figure 5.1 Internet Bandwidth Aggregation

Source: Robert E. Lee, "Caching to Relieve Bandwidth Congestion," *Sunworld*, June 1998

tion across any wide area network.[1] The Internet is the underlying application that drives the distribution of static information. As this technology grows, especially as tens of millions of nontechnical users come on-line with terabytes of personal web space, the Internet performance is likely to decline rapidly. Product developers and service providers are quick to recognize the impending disaster scenario and are responding proactively by bringing to the marketplace new web-caching products and services, including satellite datacasting services. Preliminary industry reports released on initial experiments conducted by these product developers and service providers suggest that a moderate-sized cache (0.5GB) can absorb up to 30 percent of the information requests coming from a population of 1,500 local users. The reports also indicate that further work is required to determine the impact on local user communities, the relative advantages of different caching strategies, and comparative benefits and costs.[2] With that in mind, this chapter reviews the different caching strategies for national and international access; the functionality and effectiveness of current caching systems; and the costs and benefits of different caching strategies in different situations— all in the context of determining their impact on the productivity improvement of an ISP's operations.[3]

Caching Principles

Caching migrates copies of requested objects from origin web servers to a place closer to the clients. Once an object pointed to by a URL has been cached, subsequent requests for the URL will result in the cached copy being returned, with little or no extra network traffic being generated. The cache is located on a machine on the path from multiple clients to multiple servers. The simplest example, as shown in Figure 5.2, would be that of two servers strung after another.

In principle, clients' requests for web objects are sent to a first-level cache server. That first-level cache has a sibling relation with another first-level cache and has a top-level cache as parent. If the requested object is present on the first-level cache and not out-of-date or recently modified on the original server, the object is sent to the client from the cache. Therefore, traffic for these objects is

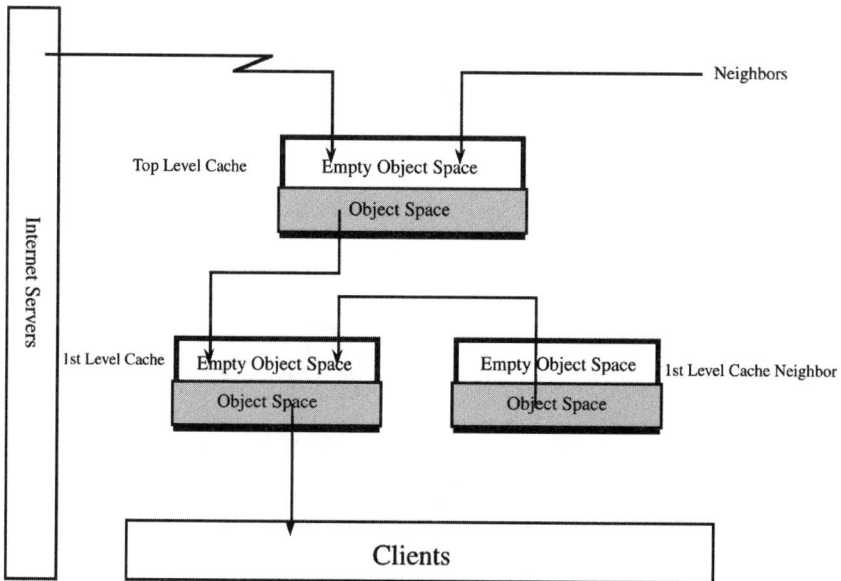

Figure 5.2 Simple Hierarchical Architecture of a Caching Mesh

Source: Adapted from Andre de Jong, Ton Verschuren, Henry Bekker, and Ingrid Melve, "Report on the Costs and Benefits of Operating Caching Services," http://www.surfnet/projects/surf-ace/caching/cb.html

restricted to the local net between the cache server and the specific client group.

If the object is not present on the first-level cache, that cache sends out a message to its siblings and parent inquiring whether the requested object is available on one of those caches. These requests follow the Internet Cache Protocol (ICP), which is a lightweight message format used for communication among web caches. The siblings and parent send a reply to the first-level cache, following ICP, indicating whether or not the requested object is present. When the object is present at one of the neighbors or the top-level cache, the first-level cache requests the object from that cache using Transmission Control Protocol (TCP) packets. TCP uses a window size that determines the number of packets it can send to the other side before stopping for an acknowledgment. When it detects congestion, TCP reduces the window size, thereby contributing to improved system behavior.

A parent can retrieve documents from the network at the request of a hierarchically lower caching server (a child) and then send them to the child. A sibling, however, will send the documents only if they are present in its own cache. If neither the siblings nor the parent have the requested object at their disposal, the top-level cache will obtain the object from the origin web server. In this case, more expensive (e.g., international) bandwidth usually will be necessary.[4]

To work effectively, caching should ideally take place over a relatively large population of users. To accommodate such a large population of users, the principle of *cache meshes* has received much attention because of these specific advantages:

- They support many users.
- There is no need to buy a massive machine to act as the cache server.
- The cache server is located as close to the user as possible.

The terms *mesh* and *hierarchy* are often used interchangeably. To some, the term *mesh* denotes configurations where all caches are siblings and/or mutual parents of one another. Figure 5.3 elaborates on the principle and scope of Figure 5.2 to illustrate the concept of cache meshes.

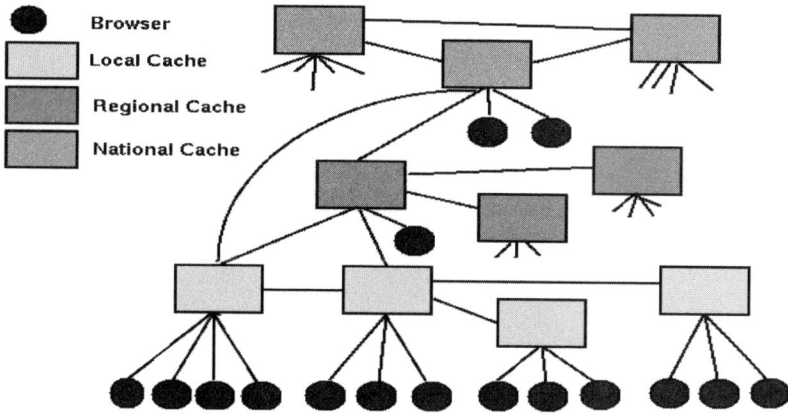

Figure 5.3 Concept of a Cache Mesh

Source: Jon Knight and Martin Hamilton, "Caching in On Caching,"
http://www.ariadne.ac.uk/issue4/caching

In the cache mesh model, when a user presents the browser with a URL (or follows a hyperlink), the browser first checks its local disk cache. If the requested URL is not found there, the browser sends a request for it to the local cache server. If the local cache server has a cached copy, it returns the copy immediately; if not, it sends a request to its neighboring caches in the network to inquire whether they have a copy of the resource. If none of them do, the browser sends out inquiries to more powerful regional and/or national cache servers located close to the physical network boundaries between Internet Service Providers and/or countries.

Although this approach may seem long and circuitous, the entire operation is efficient, compared with the many delays experienced in handling transoceanic and transcontinental web requests. To ensure that future accesses to the resource will be even faster, a copy of the returned resource is cached in the parent, regional, or national cache; the local organizational cache server; and the browser's disk cache. As mentioned earlier, some analysts prefer to define these cache meshes as cache hierarchies to underscore their treelike structure of children, parents, and grandparents. Figure 5.4 depicts the basic design concept. Although the entire complexity cannot be covered in this book, the interested reader may find the literature referenced for this chapter use-

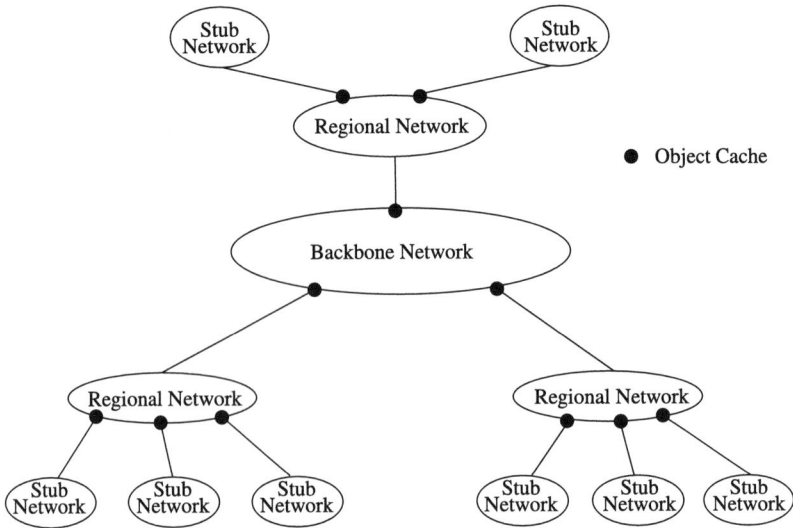

Figure 5.4 Hierarchical Cache Arrangement

Source: Danzig, B., Worrell, K., Schwartz, M., Chankhunthod, A., Neerdaels, C., "A Hierarchical Internet Object Cache," *Technical Report CU-CS-766-95, University of Colorado, Boulder, March 1995,* as referenced in Margaret Dumont, Seminar Paper Survey of Worldwide Caching, University of British Columbia, http://www.cs.ubc.ca/spider/dumont/caching/caching.html

ful. One additional benefit of hierarchical caching is that it distributes load away from the server hot spots that have popular globally accessed objects, thereby reducing latency.[5]

Out to the Internet

Internet Service Providers (ISPs) value caching because it improves the response and performance of their networks.[6] Cached data are typically served in milliseconds, as compared with a few seconds for uncached data. Caching facilitates faster web access, thereby allowing ISPs to offer differentiated services. The bandwidth reduction due to caching also results in cost savings. ISPs are using this saved bandwidth to generate additional revenue by adding more users.

As the number of users increases, several top-tier ISPs are implementing high-end web-caching software and hardware solutions. They are also candidates for using datacasting services, provided these services can live up to their promises. Next on the agenda are the low-end web-caching thin servers for regional and local ISPs, since local caching is a critical part of their business plans.

The market looks promising for local, regional, and national web-cache services, provided the interaction of the local content caching is balanced properly with the servers on which popular web content originates. The interaction issue raises a question about the reliability of the cache. If a page of content is dynamic in nature and the caching server determines that this page is frequently retrieved, perhaps that page should be pre-fetched by the caching server during slower periods of traffic, maximizing the use of bandwidth. This issue has opened the door to innovative solutions that extend beyond the local ISPs, since they may lack the resources necessary to cache enough of the Internet to meet a user community's needs. Underlying these solutions is the concept of cache hit rate, which is used to measure and trace the number of total TCP requests for web objects on the cache. *Hits* indicate that the requested object is present in the cache. *Misses* track the number of objects not on the cache that must be fetched from the origin server. If the object is on the cache, the time needed to deliver it to the client will be much shorter than when the object has to be fetched from the origin server. The time difference between these two situations is also important, because it is used for estimating the reduced latency.

Cache "hit rates" increase with upward changes in the size of the user bases accessing the Internet. Because ISPs have a finite user population, their cache hit rates are limited to the 30 to 40 percent range. If, however, a central cache is installed, which could be shared by a large number of customers, the likelihood of a hit is greatly increased, approaching 70 to 75 percent.

In addition to bringing the cache hit rate up to 70 percent or better, the ISPs strive toward preserving the bandwidth. They want to store the received object in a local file for further use so it won't be necessary to connect to the remote server the next time that same document is requested. This way network bandwidth is reduced, since some requests are directly satisfied from cached data. Once caching is introduced, however, how long is it possible to keep a document in the cache and still be sure that it is up-to-date?

Keeping a set of cached documents up-to-date is difficult. There is no mechanism for web servers to send updates to web clients. More important, many of the documents in the web are "living" documents that are updated at varying intervals. An approach, called the *weekly consistent cache*, monitors these updates to ensure that the cached objects are no more than 10 percent stale. The staleness factor is defined as *(now last update)/(last update–last modification)*. Most Internet users find a staleness factor of 10 percent acceptable.

When it is essential that the retrieved document be up-to-date, it is necessary to contact the remote server where the central cache is residing. As suggested earlier, before fetching a document from a regional, national, or a central cache, an automatic process of checking ensues to verify whether the document has been modified since the last access. Normally the verification process includes an *If-Modified-Since* request header. This ensures that the document will not be sent back unless it has been modified since the date and time specified. If, on the other hand, the document has been modified, it will be sent back, since the request is just a normal retrieval request. In these back-and-forth query-response systems, the overhead of making a connection is considerable. That brings us to the point of this discussion: If the regional or centralized caching services are too distant, they will be of little or no use to the ISPs, because the cost of the link or latency of the network will lower the quality of service. The final piece of Internet infrastructure should, therefore, include some innovations that meet ISPs' business for delivering superior update performance inexpensively and in real time over static update schemes.

Emerging Solutions

One-year-old SkyCache Inc. (www.skycache.com) has a unique solution that addresses ISPs' functional, performance, and cost requirements.[7] John Landry, a member of the SkyCache board and former chief technology officer for Cambridge, Massachusetts-based Lotus Development Corp., explains that web traffic is not getting jammed at the last mile; rather, it is the backbone itself that is getting clogged. SkyCache's basic premise is to bypass web bandwidth woes by caching popular pages and updating local ISPs via satellite links.[8] To implement this scheme, Sky-Cache uses Pentium-based servers running Solaris to send general statistics concerning frequently requested web pages to a central location, and creates a "master cache" of many sites. It preloads cache engines via satellite, which means the cache is uplinked to a satellite and downlinked to local ISP servers. In this way the popular sites are updated, kept closer to users, and "the congested cloud" of the Internet backbone is avoided.[9]

Tom Clark, CEO of MosquitoNet (www.mosquitonet.com), an ISP serving 4,500 residential and business subscribers in Alaska, cites his company's performance improvement after installing the first local cache engines in April 1997. MosquitoNet buys its bandwidth from a provider in Seattle at an average cost of $11,000 per month. If MosquitoNet were located in any of the lower 48 states, the company could buy its required bandwidth for $2,000 per month, and the savings from a cache engine would not be worthwhile. In Alaska, however, the company's bandwidth comes at a premium. Until there are serious reductions in that cost, the cache engine offers the best solution.

Clark claims that local cache servers have saved the company 18 to 20 percent in bandwidth costs, while handling 25 percent of all content requests from subscribers. To increase the number of hits served locally, Clark plans to work with SkyCache. Given SkyCache's satellite-based services, Clark expects that the hit rates into his company's cache engine will increase to more than 40 percent and that the service will further improve his company's bandwidth savings.[10]

In that context, satellite datacasting helps populate the cache at the local sites in a unique way. SkyCache, as mentioned earlier, uses Pentium-based servers running Solaris to send general statistics about which web pages are requested to a central location. Such statistics create a "master cache" of many sites. The company rents satellite time on commercial Ku-band satellites and beams the cache up to the satellite and back down to local ISP servers. Fifteen ISPs are beta-testing the service, and SkyCache expects to have 30+ ISPs hooked up and running by the end of 1999. ISPs receive a caching server, satellite dish, and access to the bandwidth that the dish provides. The ultimate benefit of the service is that it will enable the ISPs, Web Value-Added Resellers, and enterprise accounts to host sites with faster response time.[11–13]

For example, Freeside Communications Inc., an Austin, Texas-based ISP, put up the SkyCache system just prior to April 1998 and witnessed substantial performance improvement in terms of faster response time. Jeremy Porter, president of Freeside, explains that someone wanting to download the 1040 form does not actually hit the IRS site itself, but can access it through the Freeside's cache. An additional benefit of using web caching is that the content providers are being helped by the ISPs. Porter emphasizes that Freeside is downloading from a satellite, thereby avoiding expensive connection charges for its fractional DS3 lines, where it must pay for every bit of bandwidth used.[14]

SkyCache is providing a superior solution to a stand-alone cache and offering the following cost-saving and performance improvement options.[15]

BANDWIDTH MAXIMIZATION

SkyCache has demonstrated improved hit rates anywhere from 10 to 40 points over normal cache hit rates; for example, if an ISP gets a 19 percent cache hit rate, SkyCache can increase that hit rate to a range of between 30 and 60 percent. In addition, the company promotes a full Usenet News feed delivered by the same satellite datacasting technology. SkyCache claims this provides additional bandwidth conservation. The bottom line is that, with higher cache hit rates reducing load on existing circuits, an ISP can add more users and/or leased lines to its existing business before having to buy another T1 or T3.

CUSTOMER PERFORMANCE IMPROVEMENT

With its combination of patent-pending Reactive Caching technology and repopulation, SkyCache is able to deliver superior update performance in real time over static update schemes. Frequently accessed web pages are delivered directly to the cache via satellite broadcast before customers request them, enabling them to get content at higher LAN speeds (10 Mb or greater), rather than facing delays at an overtaxed web server, at a congested NAP (National Access Point), or at another bottleneck.

REACTIVE CACHING: HIGH SPEED

In general, the more people using a cache, the higher the hit rate on the cache. The innovation that SkyCache's Reactive Caching technology provides is that it will merge statistics from all of its customers to build a superior cache community. It will produce cache statistics greater than any individual customer cache could develop on its own. Everyone benefits from better statistics, because these help generate better hit rates on their caches.

Reactive Caching, by working in real time with data collected across the Internet, immediately responds to sudden bursts in web transaction activity and puts out "hot spots" caused by unexpected surges to web sites.[16] One of Reactive Caching's first successes was catching the surge upon Apple's iMac announcement.

SATELLITE BROADCAST: LOW DRAG

To realize full savings, it is not enough just to have a large cache community; an ISP must quickly update each individual cache. Satellite broadcast provides a one-way high-speed pipe to update every cache immediately and simultaneously without expensive Internet engineering. Keeping the traffic off the Net helps speed up the Net and the customer's connection to the Net.

FUTURE GROWTH

SkyCache's high-speed multi-megabit satellite datacasting technology provides a means to distribute any sort of data, including software, databases, audio, and video. Bandwidth-intensive contents such as streaming media and push channels are especially suited for transmission through future versions of SkyCache.

Multicast Internet Caching and Replication System

Another satellite-based approach to giving users access to web content has been announced by INTELSAT, which owns and operates a global communications satellite system. The INTELSAT system, with its broad global coverage, is intrinsically well suited for the service opportunities that data multicasting creates. When people think of multicasting, they usually think of broadcast-based multimedia applications, but the extent of applications that multicast can enable in today's environment includes caching web-site updates sent to distributed replication/caching sites.[17] INTELSAT's Multicast Internet Caching and Replication System is, therefore, a very timely service announcement, since it addresses packaging web content with a unique delivery service in a systematic way.[18] It will play an important role in the future of the Internet content delivery systems, which are maintained on a point-to-point basis.

The INTELSAT Multicast System will operate using standard transmission techniques. Efforts are focused on an international pilot service demonstration of a prototype for the Multicast Internet Caching and Replication System and advancing architectural models of global warehouse-kiosk cooperative web caching. INTELSAT will make a commercial system available after the completion of the pilot tests and specific commercial customization of the prototype. The system will initially use a non-IP-based multicast technology, but the subsequent phases of the system will offer INTELSAT's growing number of ISP customers a unique combination of both multicast and direct Internet content access. Because this INTELSAT system represents an introduction to multicast technology, it is important to identify and describe the multicast specific issues involved with developing applications.

IP multicast has been under development since the early 1990s, pointing to an important advance in IP, the internetworking protocol used on the Internet. It has received broad industry support as an efficient, standards-based solution for sending one copy of information to a group address so that the information reaches all recipients who want to receive it. This transmission facility works well in the ISP environment, because the ISPs are able to leverage more value from their network investment. Without multicasting, the same information must either be carried over the network multiple times (one transmission for each recipient) or broadcast to everyone on the network, consuming unnecessary bandwidth and processing and/or limiting the number of participants. IP multicasting involves groups of receivers that participate in multicast sessions: Only those receivers in a group actually receive the traffic for that group's session. IP multicast technologies address the needed mechanisms at different levels in the network and internetworking infrastructure to efficiently handle group communications.

Currently, the ISPs are beginning to employ IP multicast technologies to replicate databases and web site information across distributed server architectures with a view to achieving cost savings in network and server resources. Figures 5.5 and 5.6 illustrate how replication through multicasting amounts to savings in bandwidth and lower latencies.

National ISP Digex Inc. (www.digex.net) has taken a step toward replication by deploying transparent web caching across its network. In this context, the live Multicast Internet Caching and Replication System testing that INTELSAT began in early 1999, assumes a new degree of importance. It has demonstrated the technical feasibility of multicasting the most frequently accessed web-based content from an Internet warehouse via satellite to corresponding kiosk sites worldwide. Participants in the demonstration project included BT, COMSAT, EMBRATEL, France Telecom, KPN International, Telecom Authority of Cyprus/CYTANET, Telecom Egypt/IDSC, Teleglobe, and Telia.

The system consists of a warehouse that will collect content from frequently accessed world wide web (WWW) sites and transmit the content via satellite to registered cache sites (kiosks) using a multicast platform. Point-to-multipoint capabilities and the ease of implementing asymmetrical links are combined in this unique service platform. Figure

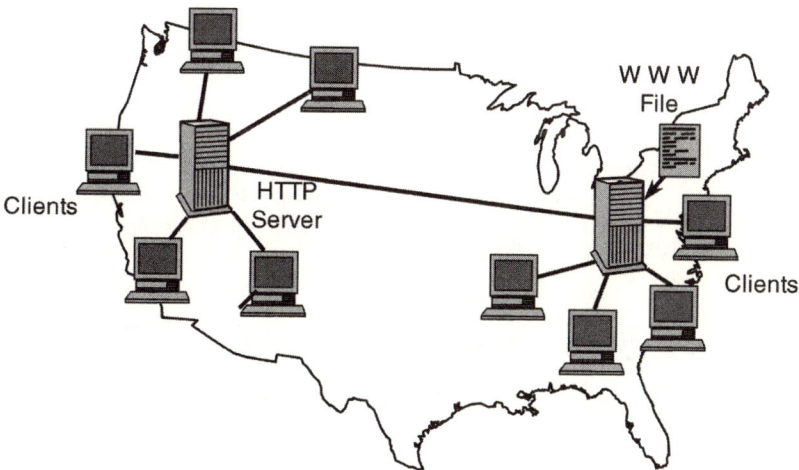

Figure 5.5 Before File Replication: Several Clients Accessing a World Wide Web File
on the East Coast

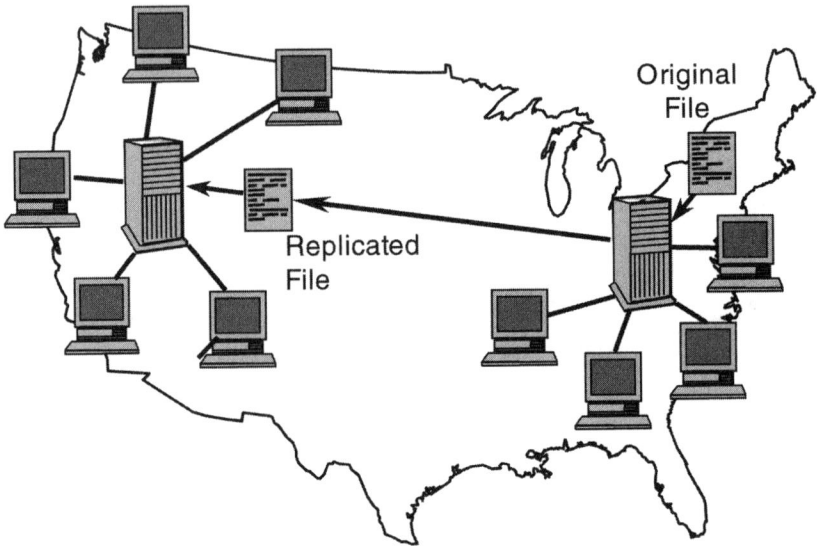

Figure 5.6 After File Replication: File Replicated on a West Coast Server Reduces Network Bandwidth and Latency Retrieval

5.7 illustrates the concept. During the field trial, Teleglobe will operate the warehouse at one of its network service facilities in Canada. The Internet content will be multicast from a primary cache at the warehouse through one of Teleglobe's INTELSAT earth stations to kiosk sites in the United Kingdom, the United States, Brazil, France, Cyprus, Egypt, the Netherlands, Canada, and Sweden. The system will provide automatic updates to Internet pages previously delivered to the kiosks. Additionally, the service will provide faster access time to Internet sites for end users, reduced international link costs for ISPs, and reduced traffic load on original Internet sites.

First Approximation to Projected Savings of the Caching Services

The costs of Internet service provision are substantial. Estimates based on several mid-level ISPs suggest that IP transport accounts for 25 to 40 percent of a typical ISP's total cost. Nevertheless, IP remains a very cost-

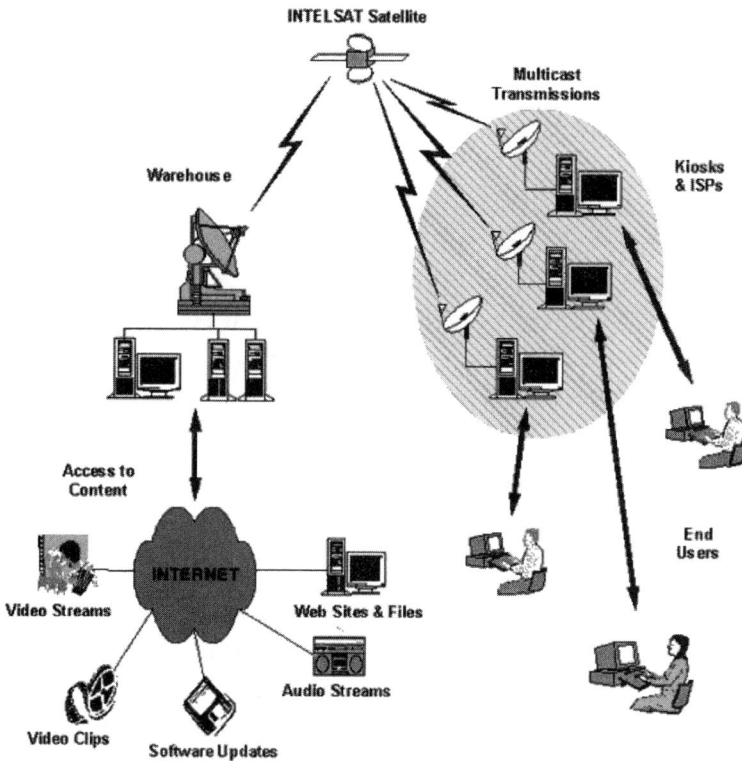

Figure 5.7 INTELSAT Multicast Internet Caching and Replication System

Source: INTELSAT, 1998, Washington, D.C.

efficient transport mechanism for applications not affected by delay, such as e-mail, file transfer, and even fax. ISPs recognize that the increase in the use of multimedia applications may result in a proportionally greater increase in the need for bandwidth.

For example, high-quality image transfer for medical applications requires considerably more bandwidth: Schemes using JPEG (Joint Photographic Experts Group) standard allow for the transfer at 56 Kbs in reasonable time. If bandwidth were essentially infinite, variations in bandwidth use would not be a problem for mechanisms such as IP that treat all packets equally. However, most ISPs pay for added bandwidth, and treat it as a scarce resource. A simple computation highlights the problem: At 300 Kbs for a video session on the Internet, it takes only

150 simultaneous sessions to congest a link on the Internet's major backbone, even with the highest-speed links. The congestion destroys some of the Internet's discipline and efficiency. Transmission Control Protocol (TCP) is used by host computers to provide a reliable byte stream to the applications that are run by an end user. TCP selects a window size, which determines the number of packets it can send to the other side before stopping for an acknowledgement. Large window sizes allow for faster throughput. With the implementation of the slow-start mechanism, TCP monitors round-trip times: If it detects congestion, it reduces the window size, thereby contributing to improved system behavior.[19] Video sessions use UDP (User Datagram Protocol). Unlike TCP, UDP does not reduce its transmission rate during periods of congestion. Users running data applications over TCP pay disproportionately in delay when video sessions congest any link. If congestion should become severe, TCP users may have an incentive to stop using the slow-start mechanism.

The tension between satisfying customers with bandwidth-intensive needs and satisfying customers with low-bandwidth applications cannot be resolved efficiently with current technology. In that context, SkyCache's datacasting and INTELSAT's Internet Multicasting and Replication System represent timely introduction of services and technologies that address not only bandwidth-intensive needs, but other requirements as well.

The rapid growth of the Internet into sectors of the economy that it was never designed to serve, such as banks and on-line information services, has revealed some gaps in capability that were unimportant to early users, but are very important to new users. These include *higher levels of customer service* and *greater reliability*. In response to these changing market needs, the nature of Internet service and the cost structures of service provision are being transformed.[20]

SkyCache and INTELSAT are still testing and evaluating their caching, and multicasting and replication systems to demonstrate how much cost reduction is possible with concomitant improvement in current data and information availability and reliability. However, they will not release their test data for public consumption in the near future. Meanwhile, results of a wide-ranging analysis of the performance of national cache verify and validate that the share of transport in total cost decreases with the implementation of caching technologies. Implementation also results in an improvement of the ISPs' overall business performance.

Most of the analysis results are available as graphs in terms of *response time, pages, cache hits,* and *cache misses,* where:

- *Response time* is the time elapsed between the cache accepting the request and the time when every byte of data has been accepted by the client. This is the actual service time.
- *Page* refers to a single request for any one item from the cache and it can be a gif, an html page, a postscript file, etc.
- *Cache hit,* as defined earlier, refers to the fact that the page requested is in the cache, fresh and unexpired.
- *Cache miss* means that the cache does not contain the page requested, and is forced to request the page from the origin server.

A selection of these graphs derived from a statistical analysis of the national cache performance in the United Kingdom is presented in this section.[21] These graphs use statistical measures, such as:

- *Mean* is the sum of all values divided by the number of values.
- *Median* is the middle value of a sorted sequence.
- *Upper Quartile* is the median of the values greater than the median; that is, 25 percent of all values are greater than this and 75 percent are less than this value.
- *Lower Quartile* is the median of the values less than the median (i.e., 25 percent of all values are less than this, and 75 percent are greater than this value).

The first graph in Figure 5.8 shows the cost effectiveness of the national cache. The direct savings being produced per day are calculated by multiplying the hit bytes per day by the current rate of charging in the UK—2 pence per megabyte. This graph shows only weekday savings to make the overall trend clearer. The current savings are approximately 600 pounds per day.

The second graph in Figure 5.9 shows the effect of the cache on overall response times. Noticeably, the response time is good, even in the upper quartile. The same response time is faster for the median

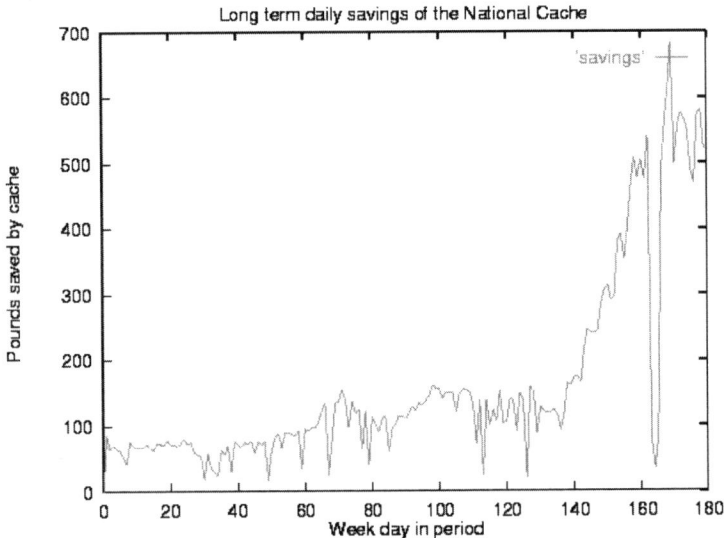

Figure 5.8 Current Savings of the National Cache

Source: Michael Sparks, "Report on a Statistical Analysis of the National Cache Performance," November 1998, http://workshop@www.cache.ja.net/Statistics/November_Graphs/Report.html

response times, especially for the lower quartile response times. The overriding concern concerning effective reliability is the cache hits. The lower quartile response time, as the graph indicates, is clearly more reliable, thereby keeping the median response time at a respectable level.

Sparks's study report produced the first iteration of comprehensive data on the efficiency and cost effectiveness of the national cache. The report notes that the national cache is a financially cost-effective solution: If extra hardware were bought to increase the hit rate by a certain percentage, it would pay for itself.

In another report on operating caching services, Andre de Jong calculated cost/benefits for:

1. A top-level cache server that has sibling relationships with other national and international ISPs.

2. A first-level cache server with clients from different organizational units connected to it.

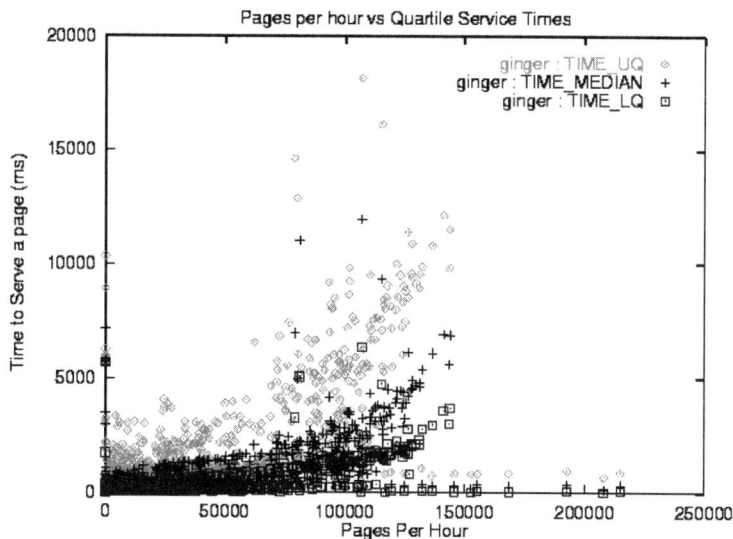

Figure 5.9 Effect of the Cache on Overall Response Times

Source: Sparks, *Ibid.*

3. A total cache mesh for a European project entitled DESIRE (Development of a European Service for Information on Research and Education).

Jong and his colleagues calculated savings by translating the hit volume of the various caches into an amount of money that represents the equivalent bandwidth not used due to caching. The results of their study indicate an 89 percent Return On Investment (ROI) for the top-level caching server, and 129 percent for the first-level server. The numbers for the total mesh yielded an ROI of 52 percent.[22] Additionally, DESIRE recorded that the reduction in latency due to caching was 79 percent. In other words, if caching was not implemented, the overall time to receive a set of objects from the net would be five times longer.[23]

To put the findings of these two reports in perspective, the benefits of a caching service are as follows:

1. A fraction of the traffic is restricted to the different network segments to which the first-level caches belong.

2. A part of the traffic is restricted to the national backbones, thereby reducing (expensive) international traffic.

3. Objects, pages, and such from the caches are delivered in a much shorter time than objects received from the origin web server because the objects are stored closer to the clients.

4. Faster response for the "misses" because caching reduces the load on the origin servers.

Further, the analyses in both instances validate that:

- Reduction of traffic means reduced need for expensive higher bandwidth on a national or international scale.
- With the reduction of traffic, there is less urgency to upgrade the international or national net to a higher bandwidth.
- Reduction of latency means saving time for the clients.
- Reduction of load on the network means less load on routers and origin web servers.

Traffic through the cache is likely to increase substantially over the coming years. In order to deal with the increased load, the effective hit rate of the national cache must be increased. SkyCache's satellite datacasting and INTELSAT's Internet Multicasting and Replication System are expected to achieve that goal. Through the use of satellites, their services are likely to outperform existing means of transmitting requests, receiving information, and refreshing cached documents through terrestrial networks. Great improvements are in store for cache hit rates, reduction of bandwidth usage, and wider availability and reliability of documents in local, regional, and national caches.[24] More realistic possibilities for managing ISP businesses efficiently and profitably have emerged, and await further implementation.[25,26] Satellite datacasting and the Internet Multicasting and Replication System are the means of achieving higher ROI in the Internet business environment.[27–29]

PART III

TAKING NEW MEASURES

CHAPTER 6

Managing Electric Utilities

Electric utilities are grappling with the challenge of a new form of cus-tomer interface that moves the utility presence from an exterior wall of a building or complex, where it is relegated to a decidedly user-unfriendly electric meter, to inside the building or complex, where it will reside in a sophisticated interactive device. This interface will serve as the key point of contact with the customer for delivering a variety of services that will extend far beyond basic energy manage-ment into automation, text message paging, electronic mail, and—depending on the sophistication of the interface—other bundled communications services.[*]

At this stage, power companies are considering a variety of forms for this interface, from an elaborate version of the thermostat to a televi-sion screen, a PC, or a telephone with a small screen that can be used to deliver a wide range of interactive services.[1]

At this writing, Southern California Edison (SCE) has nearly fin-ished development of energy management applications for the P100 screen phone manufactured by Philips, which offers Internet access,

[*] Permission to quote and reproduce tables, charts, and other materials for this chapter has been kindly granted by the EPRI Journal and Nathan Trueblood of Energy Interactive, Inc. The author gratefully acknowledges the intellectual contribution of the original investigators, researchers, authors, and presenters. If these tables, charts, and other materials explain the underlying concepts successfully, the credit goes to those original thinkers. The author is solely responsible for any mis-takes and/or omissions.

electronic mail, and electronic shopping and banking through a magnetic strip reader. With the energy management functions, users can monitor their current electricity and see how much energy their biggest appliances are consuming. The system will be tested in the homes of SCE employees. However, utilities are hesitant about the use of a screen phone interface, since no credible market test data are available to indicate how receptive the consumers are or are likely to be in using a new type of telephone for carrying out different kinds of transactions.

In 1998, Sony and Philips released set-top boxes built by WebTV that enable consumers to access the Internet through their television sets. These set-top devices connect to television sets (as VCRs do) and include receptacles for a telephone line, over which Internet data can flow, and for coaxial cable, as an option for those who prefer faster access to the world wide web. All the necessary software to hook up to and browse the Internet is built in.

Pacific Gas and Electric (PG&E) launched an innovative pilot project, enabling 50 customers in California to monitor and control their energy use through their television screens. Under a new plan, PG&E is now switching to a PC interface. Initially, this plan calls for users in 50 homes to test the use of a digital set-top box and Microsoft's "point and click" operating system to program certain appliances that would then run at specific times. To meet the overall program objectives, PG&E collaborated with TeleCommunications Inc. (TCI), the world's largest cable television operator, and Microsoft Corporation to upgrade existing cable infrastructure to a hybrid fiber-coax network.

The second phase of the project, now under way, relies on a telephone connection to the Internet, thereby requiring no new infrastructure. Participants log on to the Internet from their personal computers and access the utility's web site, using a special personal identification number to call up their own energy information. Ultimately, they will be able to pay their bills on-line.

Laurie Schneemann, PG&E's manager for the project, says that the utility is moving away from television because it tied the utility to broadband networks capable of delivering video images. Table 6.1 illustrates that the power companies have a number of media to choose from in communicating with their customers. In the new phase of the project, the utility already has a network—the Internet.

Table 6.1 Power Companies' Choices

Medium	Traditional Classification	Data Transmission Speed (bits per second)	Relative Cost	Sample Applications (with no compression)
Power line	Narrowband	30 to 20,000 (utility distribution)	Low	Remote meter reading
				Outage detection
		100 to 1 million (wiring on customer premises)	Low	Real-time pricing
Radio	Narrowband	1200 to 40,000	Low	Load control
				Security monitoring
Phone line	Wideband	Up to 56,000 (analog)	Low	Internet access
		64,000 to 6 million (digital)	Medium	Electronic mail
				Electronic billing and payment
Coaxial cable	Broadband	1 million to 15 million	Medium to high	Videoconferencing
Fiberoptic cable	Broadband	50 million to 1 billion	High	Telemedicine
				Interactive television
				Distance learning

Source: *EPRI Journal*, January/February 1997, vol. 22, no. 1: p. 9.
Available technology offers power companies a number of media to choose from in communicating with their customers, as indicated in this chart. Traditionally, these media have fit neatly into the categories of narrowband, wideband, and broadband—with narrowband technology offering data transmission capabilities, wideband offering both data and voice transmission, and broadband offering data, voice, and video.

In February 1998, Oracle demonstrated a prototype of the network computer (NC), which promises a relatively inexpensive access to the Internet. Unlike the Web TV products, the NC has a simple operating system and can retrieve any necessary applications from the Internet. According to Electric Power Research Institute (EPRI), the network computer is an ideal vehicle for bringing the electric utility inside the home. EPRI has established a formal alliance with Oracle to ensure that the device incorporates capabilities for energy management, home and business automation, and security.[2] With built-in capability for communicating with electric utilities, the extended network computer can deliver a suite of energy products and services over the Internet. David Cain, manager of new business development in the Information Systems and Telecommunications Business Unit of EPRI, points out that the users will be able to consult the NC to retrieve information and carry out transactions not only on their electricity use, but also on water and natural gas. It will have energy management features that enable customers to control several big electricity loads in their homes.

For example, a customer living in a 3,200 sq. ft. home can program the big energy users, such as air conditioners, water heaters, and clothes dryers, so that they would be most active when electricity rates are lowest. Further, the major appliances could be programmed to shut off completely during very high rate emergency periods.

In keeping with these trends, in August 1998, the U.S. Department of Energy and EPRI funded Enova Technologies, a sister company of San Diego Gas and Electric (SDG&E), to develop a user-friendly Internet-based energy management system. Under a teaming arrangement with Pacific Bell, Enova is currently developing and implementing such a system. The objective of this project, explains Tiff Nelson, the utility's project manager, "is to distinguish ourselves from other potential service providers."

There are 50 SDG&E customers participating, and they monitor and control their electricity use from their home PCs. The SDG&E system provides users the opportunity to compare any given month's energy consumption with that of the previous month and with that of the same month during the previous year. Time-of-use rates are not in place; however, users are able to control a few large appliances, and a simulated time-of-use program allows them to determine how much money they could save if such rates were implemented. This pilot program will last nine months. This project is among the first efforts to apply EPRI's Customer System 2000, which is aimed at helping utilities upgrade their web sites from browsing facilities into virtual business environments capable of supporting a variety of interactive services.

In another instance, Boston Edison announced in September 1998 that it is teaming up with RCN Inc.—a provider of integrated voice, data, video, and high-speed Internet services—to build an interactive data network for homes in 40 cities and towns in the greater Boston area. The two joint venture partners will invest about $300 million in this network development and upgrade the project over the next five years so that it can deliver energy management and other services to 650,000 customers.

On-line Utility Presence

Electric utilities are undertaking many new programs to exploit the Internet for interactive communications with customers. The Internet, including the world wide web, offers the utility industry unprecedented opportunities to deliver new products and services to the customers, while simultaneously gathering valuable market research data and information about these customers. Providing energy information valuable to customers helps a utility enter into partnership with its customers in providing total energy solutions. This in turn gives the utility company a competitive advantage over commodity suppliers of energy.

At the beginning of 1999, 180 utilities had home pages on the world wide web, but most of these are one-way communications relaying background information on their companies and news about special customer programs. Simple posting of advertising and brochures leaves much of the medium's potential for customer service untapped. The next step, therefore, should be to enhance utility companies' presences with interactive services that meet specific customer needs. Other industry sectors have already demonstrated that web sites are excellent vehicles for determining specific customer needs and addressing those needs with targeted products and services. For the utility companies, this interaction holds the key to more sophisticated energy management services, which will improve customer satisfaction, profitability, and competitiveness.

Web sites, if properly configured, will provide near-instantaneous information to customers on demand, thereby helping particular utility companies to distinguish themselves from their competition. As the wholesale power market moves toward deregulation, the issue of competition levies special requirements on the utility companies. To be competitive, these companies must maintain a real-time information system that can carry continuously updated information on transactions, transmission capacity, usage, and prices. This real-time system can be implemented through the Internet.

PG&E is enabling customers to conduct business over the Internet. Customers log onto the company's secure web site, provide answers to dynamically generated questions about their business' energy usage, and in seconds, they can receive a breakdown of their annual energy costs by end use. This breakdown illustrates the customer's annual consumption of both electricity and gas, often presented as bar charts (see Figure 6.1). Customers can also receive tips on how to save money, depending on the responses they provide. The key to providing such information is to focus on interactive applications that request input from customers before deciding on what information to provide.[3] Fig-

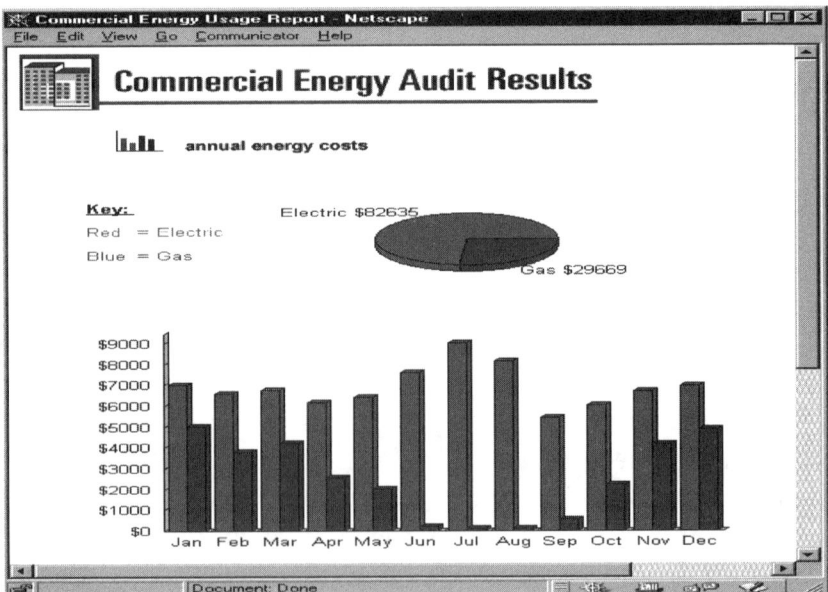

Figure 6.1 Sample Bar Chart Result of a Large Office's Energy Costs for One Year

Source: Energy Interactive, Inc. *http://www.energyinteractive.com/web.ceatablefig.html*

Figure 6.2 Real Value—Individual Customer Content

Source: Internet Strategies for Utility Companies Conference, presentation by John Powers and Nathan Trueblood, http://www.energyinteractive.com/iqpc_nash_present/iqpc.08.html

ure 6.2 depicts the type of application that is relevant and meaningful. Customers see not only generic data they could receive from existing brochures, but also information directly relevant to their own needs.[4] Customers tell the company more about themselves, and in turn the company advises them about how they can use the company's products and services more effectively.

Interactive content provides customers an opportunity to see what the utility company has to offer, even beyond the information services that brought them there. In addition, they will be providing the company with information on their behavior and preferences. By exploiting raw data on each customer, the utility company can present information unique to each visitor to its web site through secure means.

Figure 6.3 is a simplified diagram of the interactive customer applications for the web, showing how the different functions, including processing, storing, and feeding customized data/information to the customer rely on each other. There are underlying software modules that work in unison to create a successful application. It is beyond the scope of this book to go into the details that webmasters and programmers must address so that the analysis processing, database engines, and web pages seen by the customer can work together to provide customer-specific services. Figure 6.3 does not address the key issue of security. In an interactive medium, keeping a company's valuable customer data in

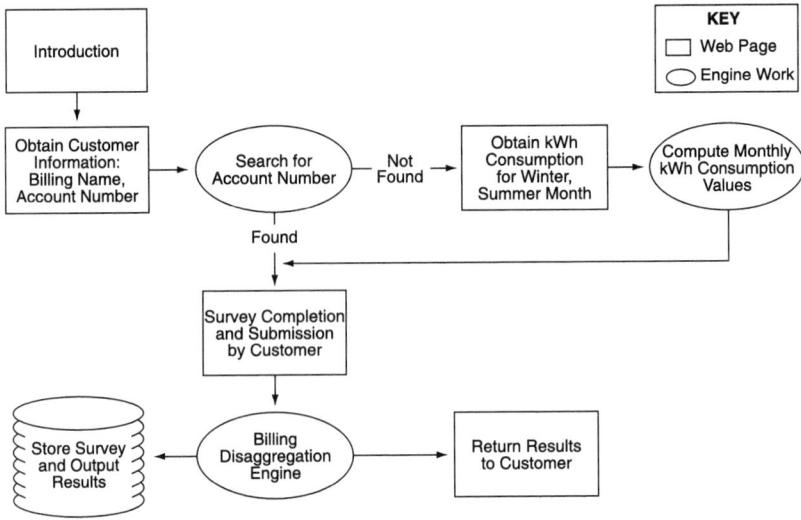

Figure 6.3 Real Value—Individual Customer Content

Source: Internet Strategies for Utility Companies Conference, presentation by John Powers and Nathan Trueblood, *http://www.energyinteractive.com/iqpc_nash_present/iqpc.08.html*

a secure environment is a major concern. Figure 6.4 illustrates a model for various hardware components of an interactive application, where company customer data is safeguarded. Every company has a variation of this model.

Customers visiting a company's web site from the Internet are allowed free access to the company's pages on the web servers. When the customer completes a form from the company's interactive application, the request goes through the firewall, the proxy server, and on to the database engine for processing. The database engine and the company's customer data reside safely within the security system. When the database engine is finished processing the request, the results are sent back to the web server for the customers to view the results in the form of graphs and tables only. No other customer information ever leaves the company site.

When customers have received valuable information and tips on their first visit, they will return to the web site again and again to rerun the energy audit, as new billing information becomes available. Table 6.2 presents a sample tabular result of a large office's energy use for one

```
┌──────────┐
│ Internet │
└──────────┘
     ↕
┌──────────┐    ┌──────────┐    ┌──────────┐    ┌──────────┐
│ Firewall │◄──►│  Proxy   │    │ Database │◄──►│ Customer │
│          │    │  Server  │    │  Server  │    │   Data   │
└──────────┘    └──────────┘    └──────────┘    └──────────┘
     ↕                 │
┌──────────┐    ┌──────────┐
│   Web    │    │ Internal │
│  Server  │    │   LAN    │
└──────────┘    └──────────┘
```

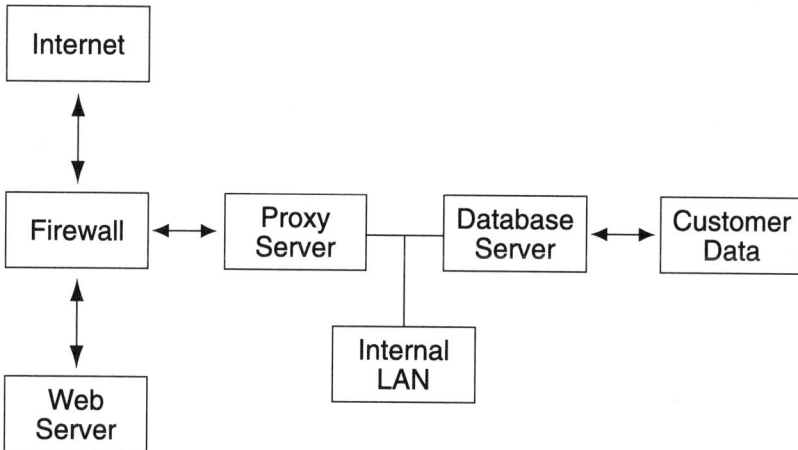

Figure 6.4 Interactive Customer Applications in a Secure Environment

Source: Internet Strategies for Utility Companies Conference, Presentation by John Powers and Nathan Trueblood, *http://www.energyinteractive.com/iqpc_nash_present/iqpc.13.html*

year. This table can be generated for each successive energy audit so that the customer can see the impact of implementing previous audit tips the next time they log on. By providing ongoing useful, actionable information, the on-line energy audit helps the company to create a favorable association with its customers, thereby increasing the value of its product. In the midst of utility deregulation, some energy providers have focused their attention on winning the residential customers as well as the larger commercial accounts. Under these circumstances, branding of utility services has become an important method for increasing the association of high-value, noncommodity service with a company.

Specific Customer Services

The audit also helps generate leads for cross-selling other products and services, including references for trade allies. For example, if a retail store manager indicates that the air-conditioning units in his store are more than 10 years old, he can be referred to an equipment supplier affiliated with a utility company and receive a discount on replacement

Table 6.2 Sample Tabular Result of a Large Office's Energy Use for One Year

```
┌─────────────────────────────────────────────────────────────────────┐
│ ※ Commercial Energy Usage Report - Netscape              _ □ ×      │
│ File  Edit  View  Go  Communicator  Help                             │
├─────────────────────────────────────────────────────────────────────┤
```

Commercial Energy Audit Results

▬▬▮▮ your energy use for the year

Appliance	Jul. Daily Cost	Jan. Daily Cost	Ave. Daily Cost	Annual Cost	Annual %	Annual Electric Usage (kWh)	Annual Gas Usage (Therms)
interior lighting	$ 76.66	$ 146.75	$ 119.65	$ 43673	39%	612511	0
heating	$ 3.04	$ 161.29	$ 81.28	$ 29669	26%	0	46048
cooling	$ 163.74	$ 0.00	$ 40.17	$ 14661	13%	197974	0
exterior lighting	$ 18.13	$ 34.70	$ 28.29	$ 10327	9%	144831	0
ventilation	$ 16.11	$ 30.84	$ 25.15	$ 9178	8%	128722	0
office equipment	$ 1.17	$ 2.23	$ 1.82	$ 664	1%	9311	0
Miscellaneous	$ 14.54	$ 11.31	$ 11.35	$ 4135	4%	57547	0
Total	$ 293.36	$ 387.09	$ 307.68	$ 112303	100%	1150892	46047

```
│ Document: Done                                                       │
└─────────────────────────────────────────────────────────────────────┘
```

Source: Energy Interactive, Inc. http://www.energyinteractive.com/web.ceatablefig.html

cooling equipment. By providing this type of useful, timely information, and fostering a one-on-one relationship, the energy audit continues to build brand equity with small business customers.

Efficiency

Getting customers to think about energy conservation can be a difficult, if not impossible task. As described earlier, the customized energy usage analysis and tips show customers how they can control their energy costs. It is one of the ways that a utility company can encourage its customers to consider issues of efficiency and conservation, while reducing the difficulty and frustration in deciphering their utility bills.

San Diego Gas & Electric (SDG&E) provides another example of how utilities are experimenting with more interactive approaches to the Internet.[5] As illustrated in Figure 6.5, from the company's home page, customers enter the Virtual Reality Greenhouse, an image of a family room in which they can click on overhead lights, a stereo, and other energy devices to find out how much electricity is consumed.

Welcome! You have come to the VR Greenhouse. It is a truly unique interactive simulation which is not only entertaining, but could help you save money on your monthly bills.

This simulation is based upon an exhibit put up by SDG&E at the county fair in which visitors entered rooms in a house designed to illustrate concepts of energy use. It was intended to give people a new perspective towards the way they use gas and electricity, and how they could use it with less expense and greater satisfaction.

We have re-created that experience here in a virtual environment. You can explore a living room and experiment with its contents. All of your actions will be taken into account by a specially created program that lets you know immediately how much energy your decisions use and how this is reflected in the amount you pay each month. Plus, there are plenty of helpful hints to assist in your decisions and you can be sure that there is a lot you might not of thought of. So, come on in and make yourself at home!

Figure 6.5 Virtual Reality Greenhouse

Source: http://www.sdge.com/vrgreen_web/

Taking Control

Gearing up for full-fledged competition among power companies, the utilities involved in the previously referenced developmental efforts believe the new services that the Internet provides can help them retain existing customers and possibly attract new ones. The web-based energy audits that save customers money on their electric bill are just the beginning. Utility companies today are more aware of the business implication of two-way communications. They have witnessed that in the conduct of their business, delivering information via the web rather than on paper has a number of advantages: It cuts down the mailing time from several weeks to a few seconds on the Internet. These time savings provide opportunities for follow-up actions. Figure 6.6 depicts the other business management benefits. For example, the web-based system is far more flexible, allowing for changes and updates to be done at a far lower cost.

The project or business management implication of that in the utility industry should be obvious: In the utility industry, data and information are increasingly the raw material used to create value, which in turn

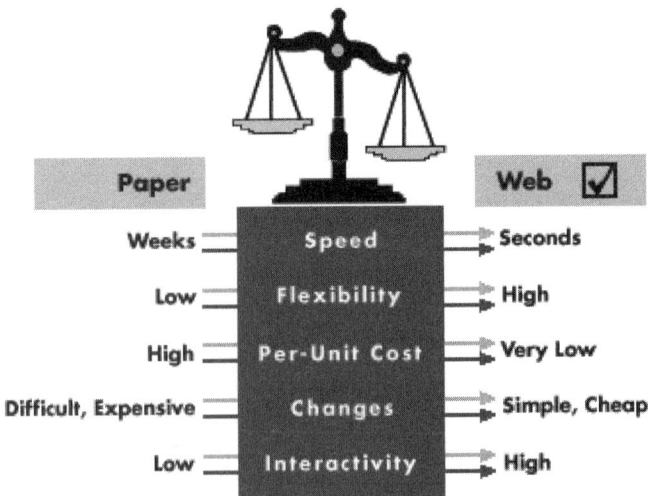

Figure 6.6 Advantages of Web-Based Interactions

Source: Internet Strategies for Utility Companies Conference, presentation by John Powers and Nathan Trueblood, *http://www.energyinteractive.com/iqpc_nash_present/iqpc.25.html*

generates revenues and puts profit on the bottom line of a company's balance sheet. One percent of the company's customer base in the utility industry represents 30 to 40 percent of its revenue, or more. In order to retain this customer base, energy service providers must deliver more than just reliable power. They will have to provide the information their customers—both residential and commercial—need to manage their energy costs. For these customers, energy services can account for a significant portion of their operating costs. Any changes in data and information, therefore, become more valuable and critical to both the energy supplier and the customer in terms of business profitability. Initially, these customers will be most affected by the use of their web browser, as they are offered new ways to:

- Analyze their own billing information and metered interval load data
- Compare energy usage
- See cost breakdowns by energy cost components
- Measure the effectiveness of various energy efficiency efforts
- Establish accurate benchmarks for energy spending
- Download energy usage data for further in-house analysis

These analyses would be difficult to replicate using conventional means. First, it takes days, even weeks, to collect the necessary data and second, the conventional means will not provide the level of detail desired. In contrast, the web site allows the company's customers to extract meaningful information from volumes of raw data instantly, over the Internet, in a secure, password-protected environment. The utility company can update the data regularly, so the customer always sees current, relevant information. This detailed information will help customers identify wasteful energy usage at their homes or at individual sites, if they are commercial or industrial customers and save them far more than just shaving a tenth of a penny off each kWh. The web-based on-line service is available to them at their convenience, 24 hours a day, seven days a week.

In addition to the charts, graphs, and reports available, the web's interactive capabilities offer additional functionalities, such as rapid rate comparison analysis and interactive data editing. In an increasingly crowded marketplace, the utility company needs to distinguish its offerings from the competition.[6] These market necessities have forced electric utilities to work closely with federal energy regulators to develop a real-time market information system for electricity trading that will carry continuously updated information on bids, transactions, available transmission capacity, spot prices, and such.[7]

The web is proving to be an excellent platform for delivering targeted, meaningful messages to inform customers of any particular utility company about its latest offerings, while the competition struggles to convey its messages.

Project Management in Other Realms

Utilities are exploring a vast array of other advanced capabilities, such as remote appliance diagnostics, home security service, and on-line bill payment, to address several other project or business management needs.[8] For example, time-of-use pricing—through which rates vary during the day to more accurately reflect the actual cost of generating and delivering power at a given time—encourages customers to shift energy use away from periods of peak demand. The result is lower power bills for the customer, which can give the utility a competitive edge. Remote meter reading, meter-tampering detection (which accounts for as much as 1 percent of utility revenues), instant information on the time and location of power outages, remote connection and disconnection of customers, and information about electricity consumption patterns are just some of the business advantages.

As the Future Unfolds

Steve Drenker, manager of EPRI's Information Systems & Telecommunications Business Unit, believes that advances in an increasingly popular and accessible Internet are going to change our lives—in a dramatic way. In the not-too-distant future, virtually everything will carry an Internet address, from telephones to gas pumps and home appliances.[9] The Internet's anticipated capability of handling an almost infinite number of addresses essentially suggests that potentially every consumer electronic product can have an Internet address. In fact, EPRI is working to establish a consortium of appliance makers and telecommunications companies to develop standard messages for communications between devices. Drenker believes there is going to be an abundance of things communicating on the Internet, and it won't be people.

At this point, no one knows precisely what an appliance's Internet address would be used for. With a lot of ideas floating around, the business opportunities for utilities promise to be significant. On the most basic level, a utility could monitor the power consumed by Internet-linked appliances and perform remote diagnostics as a billable service to the owners. But advances in sensor technologies that are now underway further increase the possibilities.[10]

EPRI is also aggressively pursuing developmental efforts in utility-related telecommunications. Drenker argues that Thomas Edison didn't want to sell kilowatthours; he wanted to sell value, such as a lighted room. But he couldn't charge for a lighted room. Now the capabilities that allow us to do this are becoming a reality.

CHAPTER 7

Taking New Measures

Making Change

During the industrial age, the control of capital was supreme, and therefore the crux of all executive decisions was the acquisition and investment of capital. The efficiency of using the capital was the accepted measure of corporate performance.* Corporations bought equipment based on their return-on-investment, and these corporations paid bonuses on the basis of return-on-assets. The shares of these corporations were valued by the stock market largely on trends on these corporations' return-on-equity.[1]

Today, it is common knowledge that the United States has made the transition from an industrial to an information age. This realization has changed our perception of technology and how it influences our day-to-day lives. Paul Strassmann, after 20 years' experience as a CIO trying to explain budget increases to corporate executives, asserts that the time has come to examine information technology as the essence of most businesses instead of just a machine tool.[2] In *How We Evaluated Productivity* and other publications (www.strassmann.com/index.html) he concludes that there is no demonstrable correlation between the financial perfor-

---

* The author gratefully acknowledges Paul Strassmann's intellectual and professional contribution to this chapter. If this chapter explains the underlying concept of Return-On-Management (ROM) successfully, the credit should go to him. The author of this chapter is solely responsible for any mistakes and/or omissions.

mance of a firm and the amount it spends on information technologies.[3–10] An improved method of defining the measurement criteria on Internet investment may very well spur on the nature and extent of investment spending in supporting business missions through caching and multicasting replication systems. It will also help measure how that investment contributed to productivity as opposed to computing the gross amount being spent and the hardware and software being acquired. More specifically, a CFO should review where the company is spending money to simply upgrade a particular process or an application, or improving a business function and thereby integrating the whole enterprise.

In the preceding chapters, companies that are upgrading information infrastructures, including their own, were profiled. In modern enterprises, the performance of high-technology and service businesses are influenced by factors other than capital itself. One of the purposes of the company profiles has been to identify these other factors and provide greater insight on more relevant and meaningful ways to define the ROI measurement criteria.

The Real Language of Business

The case materials refer to notions, which the companies have used to show the value of technology investments. First, the benefits have been stated in terms that go right to the heart of the company's most important business objectives, such as *increased market share, subscriber base, customer service,* or *profitability* to ensure that CEOs and their top managers understand the definition of the value of technology.

If the value of technology were defined purely in terms of increasing throughput, for instance, most of the CEOs of the profiled companies would have been less enthusiastic in responding to new caching and/or multicasting technology investment proposals. Instead, the technology in question has been described as enabling a company to cut time to increase market or subscription base by several months so it can overwhelm the competition. Management quickly understood the significance of that kind of an investment option.

Second, some benefits defy quantification, and it is common knowledge that the IS profession values precision. Financial experts and marketing number crunchers value numeric measures. The challenge is to find a common ground where both sides have ample scope for (a) giving consideration to soft benefits, and (b) measuring and analyzing benefits that are meaningful to general management in terms of profitability of the enterprise. It is a deadly serious exercise, but if done according to a technique described in the following section, it is possible to derive numbers that could make an honest and convincing argument.

A Resounding Maybe

The leadership team at MosquitoNet, and also Jeremy Porter at Freeside Communications decided, as outlined in Chapter 5, in favor of the Sky-Cache's caching technology deployment despite the uncertainty concerning immediate returns on investment. Their position statements indicate that in today's economy, businesses are becoming profitable because of their management and not because of capital.

Return On Investment (ROI) and other justification methods have a project authorization bias (as explained in the following paragraphs). They critically review capital budgeting with the intention of exercising maximum influence over future directions of a business. Once a capital investment is approved, the operating expenses are based on the initial investment decision. The annual costs are fixed; no major changes are possible. Management attempts to estimate expected benefits and costs for all innovation with reasonable confidence.

If this investment-oriented logic is applied to system automation or infrastructure development, it will invariably favor projects that automate existing business procedures instead of changing them to take advantage of the new information-handling methods. In this framework, emphasis tends to be on controlling new investments. In many instances, this tendency has led to the identification and establishment of the information system as a discrete and separate function, which resulted in misapplications of technology because goals and actions got confused.[11]

Proving that the desired goals have been reached is difficult assignment, especially if a proposed technology project requires unanimous approval from constituencies that have conflicting requirements, opposing interests, and diverse qualifications in considering the merits of the project. Unless there is a measurable financial outcome for an information technology project, the clarity of its goal is questionable.

When the caching and multicasting replication system is introduced into an ISP organization, its effects will be systemic, affecting the operation of the entire organization. Because the consequences will modify the way the ISP conducts its business, measurements must record the aftereffects of many changes, instead of just one isolated improvement. This raises a pertinent issue: How can one set the goals for the caching and multicasting replication technology investments? What principles help evaluate a scheme for changing systems that manage an organization? The answer is: Measure *productivity* of an enterprise before and after the caching and multicasting replication system deployment. If gains in organizational productivity are evident, one can infer that the system improved overall performance. Because ISP is an information-based enterprise, its rational choice would be to integrate the information system into every manager's job and measure management productivity instead of capital or labor productivity. ROI fails to show that the performance of high-technology and service businesses is influenced more by the quality of their management than by their assets. It can no longer explain why companies in equivalent markets, with similar capital structure, and with the same information infrastructures deliver remarkably different financial results.[12–14]

In today's dynamic environment, a CEO and a CFO need to extract business value from their investments in the caching and multicasting replication system technology. They need a methodology that clearly shows how to determine the economic profit or, economic value added (EVA), as it is being defined today. They want to show the shareholders how many dollars of net gain accrue to the shareholders for every dollar paid for management.

Keeping these points in mind, a methodology based on the concept of *return-on-management* (ROM) is presented here. The ratio is derived by first isolating the *management value-added* of an enterprise, and then dividing it by the total *management costs* of the enterprise.

To estimate the Cost of Management, the costs of Sales, General & Administrative (SG&A), and Research & Development (R&D), as reported in published financial statements, are added. The basis for this estimation method has been discussed in *Information Productivity* by Paul Strassmann (The Information Economics Press, NY, 1999). Management value-added is what remains after every contributor to an enterprise's inputs is paid. If management value-added is greater than management costs, we are justified in saying that managerial efforts are productive because the managerial outputs exceed managerial inputs. Figure 7.1 illustrates the cost elements for deriving the Management value-added.

ROM(TM) Index is therefore a function of management output and management input and it gives management productivity. Unlike other techniques, it identifies productivity of the enterprises, regardless of their size or how many professionals they employ. It has been empirically verified that ROM is the only statistic that shows a positive relationship to technology spending.

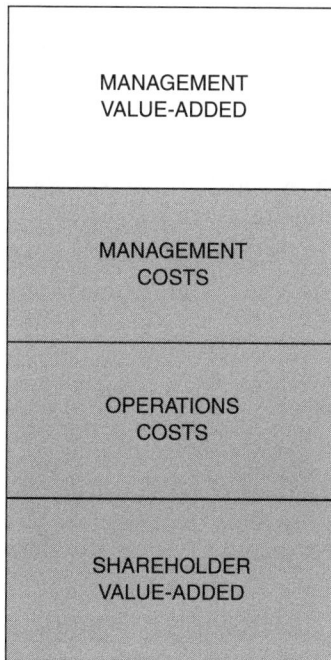

Figure 7.1 Cost Elements for Deriving the Management Value-Added

Source: Paul A. Strassmann, *Introduction to ROM Analysis: Linking Management Productivity and Information Technology*, ... ssmann.com/consulting/ROM-intro/Intro_to_ROM.html, p. 11.

Paul Strassmann examined the 1995 *Computerworld* (CW) Premier 100 companies, which ranked corporations by information productivity and compared them with the top 100 Fortune corporations, ranked by revenue. He documented that for the period from 1992 through 1994, the CW Premier 100 companies delivered 347 percent more sales growth, 334 percent more growth in shareholder equity, and 46.2 percent more employment growth, in comparison with the big 100 corporations. (See Table 7.1.) To develop the listing of the CW Premier 100 companies, Strassmann ranked 5,000 U.S. corporations by Information Productivity. His earlier work is currently being updated and the data are not yet available. The reader is advised to review Paul Strassman's web site for more current information on the information productivity rankings. Refer to www.Strassmann.com/index.html.

ROM(TM) Productivity Index relates to the numbers that are watched and understood by the board of directors, top executives, and shareholders and offers a sound basis from which to start discussions on how to improve these numbers. The Index is ideal for analyzing major investment proposals involving information technologies, such as caching and multicasting and replication system. This point is explained in more detail below.

Information (e.g., *Management*) assures survival of a firm in a competitive environment. Without continuous intervention by Management, every enterprise will suffer from chaotic conditions that occur

Table 7.1 Information Productivity (TM) Rankings, Industrial Companies

	CW Premier 100 Companies			Fortune 100 Companies		
	1992	1994	Growth (percent)	1992	1994	Growth (percent)
Net Sales	65,152,154	92,086,506	41.3	1,938,707,606	2,169,627,321	11.9
Shareholder Equity	36,522,568	56,868,252	55.7	628,033,046	732,696,463	16.7
Sales, Gen. & Admin.	11,809,902	13,707,939	16.1	497,963,151	520,523,106	4.53
Research & Development	2,901,620	3,778,062	30.2	25,239,650	22,986,013	−8.9
Employment	566,157	828,003	46.2	9,710,166	9,614,949	−1

Source: Paul A. Strassmann, Productivity, not Bigness, is Beautiful, @ Computerworld, September 19, 1995. Also refer to http://www.Strassmann.com/index.html.

when external information (about customers and competitors) and internal information fail to provide guidance about what action should be taken.[15] Through the case materials, we have already verified and validated the need for Management intervention. Now the critical task at hand is to determine how much information (Management) is necessary to run an enterprise.

Earlier we made an implicit reference to this issue. It may have become clear that central to the issue of Management is the generation of a positive *net value-added* to survive. A corporation becomes profitable only when it generates a net surplus of wealth. For auditing purposes, traditionally the corporation would evaluate the following factors annually:

Gross Return based on:

1. Additional revenue per year
2. Direct savings per year
   One-time savings
   Annual savings
3. Productivity
   Savings from processing more information electronically annually
4. Indirect savings
   Annual savings resulting from the avoidance of additional staffing, etc.

First-year total return on investment: $$$

Subsequent total annual return on investment: $$$

Costs:

1. Hardware and software costs
2. Operating system costs
   Administration costs
   Support costs
3. Application costs
   Administration costs
   Support costs

4. One-time training costs

5. First-year total enterprise costs

6. Subsequent total annual costs

First-year Net return on investment: $$$

Subsequent Net Annual return on investment: $$$

It is crucial to understand that Management has the capacity to develop an organization that extracts from the hostile environment net value-added (*outputs*) in excess of total costs (*inputs*). Because management of information is inseparable from management's general roles, thus the processing of information by a caching and multicasting replication system should be viewed as an extension of traditional management roles.

Empirical evidence suggests that the ROM Productivity Index is a technique that could be valuable in investment analysis concerning caching and multicasting and in replication system deployment. It is the only methodology that allows exploring, measuring, and quantifying the soft benefits of the caching and multicasting and replication technology by its principal customers, the managers of the ISP. The old ROI formulation can now be replaced by directly measuring the productivity of Management as an information-processing function.[16] To that end, there are some immediate analytical advantages that can be derived. The use of the caching and multicasting replication system will not be evenly distributed among workers in an enterprise. The value-added option in the ROM technique will allow an enterprise to better understand the effectiveness of the caching and multicasting and replication system by separating its managerial uses from other applications. An enterprise can then evaluate the effectiveness of *Management* with or without the caching and multicasting and replication system services. Additionally, an ISP enterprise can isolate cases showing superior managerial productivity, and then examine how their caching and multicasting and replication system uses differ from cases that show inferior managerial productivity.

Freeside Communication's approach, as outlined in Chapter 5, was to identify business objectives by department managers responsible for the IRS web site. A further refinement to that approach is to extract the perspectives of management at levels differentiated by:

- Officials
- Managers
- Professionals
- Technicians
- Skilled and unskilled workers

The mission is to do an annual audit for an ISP enterprise, including a whole company as well as operating divisions. The decision makers want the users' views on local caching efforts to justify the importance of caching investments compared with other investments. Freeside Communications or MosquitoNet would certainly want the managers to articulate how much the enterprise gains in the way of productivity by spending on the caching and multicasting and replication system not included in explicit budget items, including hardware, software, data and voice communications, supplies, and outside vendor support.

Every enterprise should insist on including these questions as part of a larger checklist for an objective, complete professional survey to be conducted by a competent outside research firm. Further, by reviewing such financial data as:

- Net sales
- Sales and general administrative expense
- Research and development expense
- Profit after taxes
- Shareholder equity, etc.

the firm will add value to the survey by benchmarking the companies' usage of the caching and multicasting and replication system against the other companies in the industry. These details will provide accurate facts and figures on the management productivity improvement due to caching and multicasting and replication system deployment. Armed with such foresight, decision makers can make more accurate caching and multicasting and replication system investment plans.

Internet Policy for the Enterprise

Put It In Writing

There can be superior and inferior managerial productivity based on the Internet use. To clarify "inferior productivity," the Internet is still going through its adolescence and has much maturing to do. Current efforts are concentrated in developing tools and finding and structuring interesting sets of information and data to view with the tools. As exciting and productive as these developments are, therein also lies the cause of concern for enterprises. While using the tools, employers may make inadvertent mistakes or deliberately mishandle information on the Internet. If and when that happens, the enterprise may face problems ranging from embarrassment, employer liability, and copyright violations, to loss of trade secrets, loss of productivity, or information overload.[1]

During the Third Annual Ernst & Young/Information Week Information Security Survey, twenty companies reported information security losses in excess of $1 million. The Internet business users that exchange information externally reported numerous successful or attempted break-ins in the past year. According to the Federal Bureau of Investigation, 80 percent of all computer crimes reported to the agency involve the use of Internet to break into computer systems.[2] Most companies express concern that they do not have proper tools, well trained personnel, or properly developed guidelines and/or policies to protect the enterprises from information (security) losses. But most of the Ernst & Young survey respondents demonstrated "growing awareness of security problems and increased willingness to devote additional resources to their solution."[3] A commanding 87 percent of Internet users stated that they would use the Internet more for business purposes if they could devise a good workable policy for security and maintenance of a productive workplace. They all agreed that as companies rely on the Internet to exchange data among remote locations, effective guidelines will be needed that could be centrally developed and uniformly enforced at all locations of an enterprise. These guidelines should address the Internet features that must be monitored for developing policy on access, use, and disclosure of information through the Internet.

Hypermedia presentation is an operational feature that needs careful monitoring. The presentation should be highly representative and descriptive of the enterprise's work. It is important to reflect an accurate, overall picture of the enterprise and guard against the possibility of letting anyone produce and publish anything that is piecemeal, misleading, or incomplete.[4] There is a preference here for management approval and authorization of the content of enterprise information for Internet use. Management approval and authorization is an enforcement issue that deals primarily with rules governing a particular type of information. Agreement on rules is best arrived at by negotiation with those most knowledgeable about particular data and information and how they should be structured and presented in an online, hypermedia environment. The details need to be developed by the joint efforts of many people from different sources within an enterprise. The origin and control of information content might very well be at the enterprise's grass roots level. If a mechanism is put in place that brings all the relevant (technical) people together, the rules concerning security, authentication, link management, markup language standards, etc. could be properly developed, updated on a regular basis, and satisfactorily applied toward drafting and interpreting an enterprisewide Internet policy. The mechanism is beneficial to the policy process in that it is more likely to produce a policy consistent with the enterprise's business goals and strategies. It will involve successful collaboration among executives from IS, security, human resources, legal, marketing, pricing, advertising, customer relations, government affairs, purchasing, research, and operations. This involvement will have a far reaching impact on decisions regarding the policy to be adopted. The different representatives will be able to articulate their individual and collective experiences in controlling and decontrolling access to external/internal information and managing advertising, promotion, marketing, and electronic commerce-related Internet transmissions. Collective awareness will facilitate a clear, wise, and sophisticated understanding of the issues that will produce a "workable" strategy document.

Caution

"You can't just put equipment out there and let people use it for illegal purposes."[5]

Attorney Helena Kobrin

Once the policy is baselined, it should be distributed to all layers of management within an enterprise. It will inform everybody what needs to be done to reduce security losses, including disciplinary actions that must be taken in case of policy violations. It will also have a substantial impact on advising management that personal authority and accountability matters most in presenting the enterprise and its activities appropriately to the public. When the policy document promulgates professional standards of conduct, it is likely to spur creative individual use of the Internet resources, while furnishing guidelines for the most appropriate, efficient, and safe usage of Internet resources.

Enterprise Functions and Suggested Policies

Companies may have their own home page. This home page is the company's own proprietary document. As such, what goes on behind the scene to create, manage, review, modify, and change with a view to keeping the page current, should be handled carefully, seriously, and with a sense of urgency. More specifically, there are three *tactical* problems that the CEOs/CFOs/CIOs must address: how to get a handle on what goes on over the Internet, how to identify the risks, and how to minimize the legal and management costs of doing business on the Internet. Additionally, the CIO often has a strategic challenge of being a "visionary" toward the tasks of aligning business and technology goals and implementing sound enterprise Internet policies.

Enterprise strategies are those practices that result in "guidelines and policies" that impact how Internet use and support processes are conducted. Table A.1 provides a high-level breakdown of management strategies that reflect a philosophy and methodology based on extensive experience in addressing enterprisewide Internet issues.[6] It begins with a listing of the component functions associated with the purpose of the enterprise's Internet project. The core strategies, if implemented, will provide an opportunity for an enterprise to achieve a collaborative relationship among the various divisions and also maintain bottom line Internet objectives of service quality, customer satisfaction, risk management, and legal cost control. Based on this outline, Acceptable Use Policy (AUP) framework,[7] and reviews of several other interim guidelines prepared by such agencies as the National Institute of Standards and Technology, an illustrative example of Internet policy is presented here. The hypothetical company is RB Enterprises. This is a starting place for developing a coherent policy on Enterprise Internet use. It should be viewed as a useful resource, but not the final authority. Different enterprises will have different resources and rules and this piece *cannot* cover every enterprise and its various jurisdictions. Instead, the purpose here is to define a lasting statement of what an enterprise's intent is toward the Internet.[8] Further, the audience for this work is comprised of decision makers (CEOs/CFOs/CIOs) and, in this instance, middle management and system administrators. This work is not directed at engineers or programmers who are trying to deploy the Internet with secure programs. Rather, the focus here is on policies and procedures that must be in place to support the Internet services that an enterprise may be implementing.

An important feature for policy making is a long-term look at Internet use—what will be the enterprise's relation to the Internet in five or fifteen years? A broad policy statement will allow the enterprise to keep the original policy statement unchanged for a reasonably long period, but its implementation will always be subject to change. For

Table A.1 Enterprise Internet Policy Outline

Internet: Management Strategies

Purpose of the Enterprise Internet Project
Marketing on the Internet
Selling on the Internet
Facilitating markets on the Internet
Disseminating information on the Internet
◆
Effective and Efficient Usage
Mandatory training requirements
Moderating/Monitoring/Participating in USENET/Electronic discussion groups
Qualifications for access authority
Handling "advertising," lead generation
Professional standards in posts—disclaimers
Web pages must professionally represent enterprise
◆
Classes of Mail Allowed
Casual Communications
"Official Correspondence"
◆
Restrictions on Nonprofessional Usage
Inappropriate humor, graphics/images, chain letters
◆
Protecting Proprietary Information
Proprietary information sharing restrictions
Uploading/downloading copyrighted materials
◆
Security Awareness
"Rogue" and "back door" Internet connections
Firewall policies
◆
Virus Awareness
Risks of downloads
Problems of virus scanning
◆
Support Resources
Who authorizes usage
Who maintains Web presence
◆
Disciplinary Actions for Policy Violations
◆
Policy Review Committee Representatives
◆
Appendix: Netiquette Tutorial
◆
Inclusions by Reference: Corporate e-mail and Security Policies

instance, a broad policy statement articulates what is acceptable and unacceptable use of the Internet. At extreme ends, it is fairly clear what the issues are, but issues at the center are harder to define. For example, at what point is sending e-mail by Internet to a friend too far from being acceptable? Those gray areas are left to the discretion of the key enterprise executives.

As the Internet practices grow and officials are assured that the enterprise's reputation, proprietary information, software or similar other interests are not being compromised, some concessions for private e-mail use or similar uses may be made. The productivity/ Internet relationship is always going to be a major concern for the enterprises.[9] It is incumbent upon each enterprise to put any area off limits and that essentially is the implementation strategy angle that the senior management, HR, legal counsel, employee users, security, union representatives, the MIS director, and the CIO of an enterprise must tackle. If the illustrative material aids in the actual development of an Internet Implementation Policy, this section of the book will have served its purpose.

RB Enterprises' Internet Policy Directive

PURPOSE OF THE ENTERPRISE INTERNET PROJECT

This term Internet refers to the world wide web (WWW), bulletin boards, anonymous file transfer protocol (FTP), and other services. Much has been written lately about the Internet, its components, and the emerging commercial advantages these services and features offer. With all this attention, it is important to evaluate the potential of the Internet and seize the opportunity to exploit its commercial advantages. Since the Internet provides access across a number of interconnected networks, information on a server directly connected to the Internet is available to everyone on the Internet. Information that is placed on the Internet must, therefore, be cleared through appropriate channels as other publicly released material.

The purpose of the Enterprise Internet project is to develop a policy for using the Internet as a transmission media to distribute information both inside and outside the enterprise. The following is released as an Interim Policy and remains in effect until superseded by a formal fully coordinated Enterprise Internet Policy. This Interim Policy acknowledges the complex and explosive growth of the Internet technology which the company plans to leverage with the initial focus being given to the following areas.[10]

Marketing on the Internet

The company will authorize marketing activities over the Internet, subject to appropriate coordination and supervision by the respective department heads. These activities will take any of several forms.

First, the Internet will be used as a medium for advertising. Interactive sales-related marketing information will be provided over the Internet, especially for big-ticket items, so that the consumers get as much information as possible before committing to a purchase.

Secondly, the company will leverage the interactivity and multilayered nature of a web site to learn about the different information accessed by different groups of online consumers and recycle this information back into the future marketing efforts.

Also, the company will market to commercial accounts over the Internet. It will distribute technical product information, including technical specification and a host of related product data, to commercial customers, subject to appropriate departmental authorization.

Selling on the Internet

The company will offer goods through online catalogs, use electronic order forms, and furnish shipping and credit card information while online.

The company will make sales to commercial accounts over the Internet. It will use the Internet to exchange information, such as bidding documents and sales orders, with the suppliers, subject to supervision and approval by the supervisory and management staff of the appropriate department.

Facilitating Markets on the Internet

The company will leverage the various Internet facilities: "smart agents," virtual mall, and Internet directories. In the business-to-business context, the company will use private procurement systems to establish links to proprietary computer networks as business warrants expansion along those lines.

Disseminating Information on the Internet

As noted under Marketing on the Internet, the company will provide information on the Internet, under supervision and control of senior management, to enable consumers make better informed purchasing decisions.

EFFECTIVE AND EFFICIENT USE

This section promulgates Internet usage policy guidance to satisfy new and changing legal and management issues.

Mandatory Training Requirements

The law regarding the intersection of legal issues and Internet technology is emerging, but as the company plans to leverage the Internet for commercial gains, it must minimize its potential legal exposure.[11]

The company shall mandate that all employees undergo training on Internet productivity and etiquette.

The corporate training department will coordinate training schedules with the other line of business units.

The training will be updated and repeated as often as is deemed necessary by the supervisory and management staff.

For the benefit of all employees, the training will be comprehensive.

It will instruct the employees about the restrictions that apply for Internet e-mail, games, or browsing for personal reasons.

It will instruct the employees about the company's risk of defamation claims and provide necessary guidelines for employees who have specific business to conduct in chat channels and bulletin boards.

It will instruct employees about the prohibition of and ramifications for unauthorized use of the Internet or bulletin boards, sharing of confidential passwords, or downloading and installing software.

Upon satisfactory conclusion of the training, each employee shall sign and return an employee agreement and corporate Internet policy to the respective department manager for his/her cognizance. The manager will submit that to HR for record keeping.

Moderating/Monitoring/Participating in Electronic Discussion/USENET Groups

To avoid facing liability, RB Enterprises expressly prohibits all employees and/or third parties from using Internet system with an account bearing the enterprise ".com" domain name to moderate, monitor, or participate in moderated or unmoderated bulletin boards ("BBS"), listservs, chat groups, forums, or other "online cocktail parties."

If and when special needs arise, the respective supervisory personnel and department managers will review and approve individual participation requests on a case by case basis.

RB Enterprises mandates the use of the following outbound e-mail and discussion disclaimers:

> "This message represents the personal views and opinions of the individual sender and should in no way be construed as an authorized communication on behalf of RB Enterprises."[12]

Qualifications for Access Authority

RB Enterprises' staff will be authorized to fully use the Internet services and facilities, where feasible, as a mechanism for making enterprise-acquired data resources broadly available to the public. However, all employees must adhere to the administrative policies and procedures that have been devised for Internet services, including limitations on the use of the Internet for those activities that support RB Enterprises' business missions.

RB Enterprises reserves the right to monitor, review, and regulate usage of the Internet and any of its services to ensure that the enterprise policy is followed, services are used purely for business purposes, and RB Enterprises' rights are protected.

The employees are responsible for keeping their access codes and passwords. The employees shall never give out the access codes and passwords to anybody. If anyone asks for an employee's access code and/or password, the employee must refuse and report the incident to the IS department.

Only the director of the IS and the legal department shall have access to all employee access codes and passwords. They will have the authority to revoke a user's access code and password in the event of a perceived danger to the continued operation of a system, its integrity, or risk to the user community.

Handling "Advertising," Lead Generation

RB Enterprises will use the Internet as another medium for advertising. It will exhibit caution because there are virtually no restrictions on the amount of information transmitted and the feedback that can be received via the Internet.[13]

While advertising on the Internet, RB Enterprises shall use particular care about the information being disseminated. The traditional legal risks of advertising, namely copyright and trademark infringement, deceptive practices, consumer protection, defamation, privacy, publicity, and trade or product disparagement are also in effect in the Internet medium.

Additionally, if RB Enterprises provides "hyperlinks" in its online advertising, which will allow the user to go from one page to a totally independent page containing actionable (e.g., false, defamatory, deceptive) content on the jumped-to page, it increases RB Enterprises' legal exposure. As RB Enterprises turns to the Internet—more specifically, to the world wide web—to advertise, all advertising materials shall be cleared through the respective department's supervisory and management staff before being placed on the Internet.

Under authority of RB Enterprises' supervisory and management staff, the enterprise will post product information in the form of text, pictures, and interactive activities including short movies, if and when such advertising adds value to the campaign.

RB Enterprises will track the frequency and manner in which different consumers navigate through the information and thus gather data for future marketing campaigns.

Professional Standards in Posts—Disclaimers

Refer to the example under subsection Moderating/Monitoring/Participating in Electronic Discussion/USENET Groups.

Web pages must professionally represent enterprise.

RB Enterprises' public face is its web page(s) and it mandates that management shall ensure that the published information on the web page(s) is up-to-date, consistent, accurate, and properly integrated with other referenced materials, including audio and video. It further mandates the management to institute a procedure for regular continual review of the enterprise's web page(s) for quality and accuracy.

RB Enterprises will invest in the web to disseminate information deemed useful by the public. Accordingly, its policy states that all employees will have collective responsibility for quality control of the material the enterprise publishes. It further instructs that as employees develop good representative literature on the enterprise and its products and services, they shall adhere to the house styles.

Management will create an Enterprise-level System Administration (WebMaster) function which will:

1. Oversee information on the RB Enterprises' WWW Internet in coordination with other senior executives
2. Provide organizational structure guidance for all RB Enterprises' WWW Internet pages
3. Review and validate RB Enterprises' WWW Internet requirements to add features and services to the Internet system
4. Maintain an RB Enterprise WWW House Style Guidelines document or set of documents
5. Provide oversight of the RB Enterprises' Guidelines Document

RB Enterprises management will create an Organizational-level System Administration (WebMaster) function which will:

1. Address overall management of the Organizational/Functional Pages and/or Server
2. Address management of the information on the RB Enterprises' server, directory, or pages

3. Address configuration management and system integrity for the RB Enterprises' Internet pages

4. Review and validate the organizational/functional Internet requirements with the RB Enterprises' WebMaster to add features and services requested to be placed on the RB Enterprises' WWW Internet system

5. Ensure that the organizational/functional information is current, consistent, and valid

6. Check to verify that the links are operational and all outages are corrected

7. Advise RB Enterprises' WebMaster on advanced planning for further development, enhancements, or upgrades

CLASSES OF MAIL ALLOWED

RB Enterprises will use the Internet to keep departments, work groups, and individuals in close contact. It recognizes that e-mail is the primary way that people on the Internet communicate with each other. It acknowledges that many people become more communicative because they prefer sending e-mail to talking on the phone or sending letters by U.S. postal service. RB Enterprises' e-mail policy is that the enterprise will use e-mail to convey direct messages that can be answered quickly and pertain to a specific workplace task. It is not just another way to talk to someone. To define the entire scope of this e-mail policy, RB Enterprises makes specific references to:

Casual Communications

E-Mail is not conversation and it does not convey emotion well, but it is recorded and can easily be duplicated.[14] While e-mail may be less formal than a hard copy letter, it is more permanent than speaking to someone on the phone. In the event of a litigation, it may be subject to discovery. Employees should take this possibility under advisement when sending e-mail both within and outside of the company. RB Enterprises' guidelines in this matter are:

1. Formulate your message correctly.

2. Use telephone when appropriate.

3. Use separate bulletin boards so people do not interfere with other people's work.[15]

4. Do not use e-mail for unrelated advertising.

5. Do not use e-mail for casual communications concerning events such as golf tournaments, garage sales, girl scout cookies, fund raisers, or "puppies for sale."[16]

Official Correspondence

Internal or external e-mail messages shall be treated as business records. RB Enterprises requires that all employees practice good record keeping. This will protect the employees in terms of their ability to prove the contents of a communication or that the information was actually sent or received, should the need arise.

1. The Records Retention Policy that is in place for paper filing applies to business e-mail in terms of how long the records should be protected and when these could be destroyed; therefore, all employees shall file business e-mail either electronically or print and place them in the paper files.

2. All employees shall keep these files organized and up to date at all times.

3. Employees shall not send courtesy copies of an e-mail message to people, unless these people have a need to view a particular message.

4. Employees shall not forward e-mail messages unless the original sender knows that the message may be forwarded.

5. Employees are not required to acknowledge an e-mail just to inform the sender that they have received it.

6. RB Enterprises' line managers who notice excessive charges for their group's e-mail account shall be authorized to request a detailed account of all e-mail transactions to ascertain who is sending messages to whom.

7. RB Enterprises reserves rights to monitor and review e-mail messages to ensure that the employees are adhering to the enterprise policy and to revise the existing policy guidelines regarding use and the potential risks and consequences of misuse of e-mail services.

RESTRICTIONS ON NONPROFESSIONAL USAGE

A variety of communication icons have evolved to express humor, sarcasm, surprise, anger, or bewilderment and these have found popular use on the Internet. Some of these have been developed so that the reader will better understand the intent and context of the message, rather than taking it the wrong way. There are also some abbreviations that are supposed to be commonly understood. Notwithstanding the cautions and clues people ascribe to the unique character of the Internet, RB Enterprises takes the position that every transmission over a computer network is potentially a communication of sorts. A communication could be defamatory if someone claims it has adversely affected his or her reputation. Some forms of communication are considered so injurious by nature that proof of damages will not be required. For the protection of all employees and its own interests, RB Enterprises shall be governed by the following guidelines.

Inappropriate Humor, Graphics/Images, Chain Letters

The Internet links many different communities with many different standards. In the eye of the law, when one set of standards that is acceptable for one community is sent by computer transmission into another community that is guided by another set of standards, the recipient community's standards prevail. As Internet users, RB Enterprises' employees must always be mindful of how their words may be interpreted and how they may be held liable for inappropriate humor, graphics/images, and/or chain letters. As such, they shall refrain from:

1. Sending, displaying, or printing sexually explicit or suggestive images;
2. Using objectionable language in both public and private messages;

3. Sending chain letters that could cause congestion and disruption of networks and systems.

PROTECTING PROPRIETARY INFORMATION

RB Enterprises equates the Internet with "public access." Its policy is that transmitting or providing access to company proprietary technical data over the Internet is tantamount to unauthorized disclosure. Such data will reveal information in violation of contractual obligations or release product details that prematurely affect the company's stock price.

Further, the policy states that no employees should transmit any unencrypted, company confidential technical information over the Internet unless it has been approved by cognizant management staff for public release by attaching appropriate distribution statement(s). Access to databases containing restricted data should not be granted over the Internet. To ensure that the employees clearly understand and adhere to these policies, the following procedural guidelines shall remain in effect until further notice.

Proprietary Information Sharing Restrictions

RB Enterprises shall release information to the public through the Internet only as necessary to safeguard information requiring protection in accordance with its established business programs, strategies, and goals. Its management shall implement the provisions of this policy by:

1. Issuing instructions for the internal administration/enforcement of the requirements prescribed herein.
2. Forwarding information proposed for release over the Internet to appropriate supervisory and management personnel for clearance and including specific recommendations concerning the material being submitted for review and concurrence.

Uploading/Downloading Copyrighted Materials

RB Enterprises will engage in digitizing its products and services to allow consumers to download the contents of their desired purchase(s) directly from the Internet. It is cognizant of the fact that the law is undeveloped in the matter of online distribution of digitized products.[17]

As RB Enterprises plans the future distribution of demos, updates, patches, and, in certain cases, full product over the Internet, it mandates that all employees become familiar with the potential antitrust and unfair competition claims, franchise questions, and other distribution laws involving copyright, patent, and trademark issues. Also, before placing any of its digitized products for online distribution, RB Enterprises must meet all provisions of the United States export laws. To avoid any possibility of wrongdoing in above matters, any RB Enterprises' employees transmitting or receiving products online must adhere to the following directives:

Uploading software

1. Review licensing and intellectual property policies prior to making software universally available
2. Seek RB Enterprises' supervisory and management personnel and legal affairs' concurrence and approval in ascertaining the scope of potential audience as well as particular laws of jurisdictions in which software will be made available

Downloading software

1. Seek RB Enterprises' supervisory and management personnel and legal affairs concurrence and approval in ascertaining licensing and intellectual property restrictions on use or dissemination of product, if any

SECURITY AWARENESS

RB Enterprises recognizes the vulnerability of existing security software and will use every precaution necessary to safeguard its confidential information before placing it on the Internet.

This section does not address how to design or implement secure systems or programs. Rather, the focus here is on policies and procedures that need to be developed to support the technical security features. This section is addressed to the enterprise management, and promulgates the following policy guidance to satisfy changing Internet-related security concerns:[18]

1. Information to be protected
2. Threats to information security
3. Likelihood of threats
4. Measures that will protect the enterprise's assets in a cost-effective manner
5. Continual process review and improvement

Enterprise management shall pay close attention to items 4 and 5, while monitoring:

Firewall Policies

Management will decide what firewall mechanism is appropriate: blocking traffic or permitting traffic. The fundamental concern of RB Enterprises' firewall policies is to protect against unauthenticated interactive logins from the "outside" world.

"Rogue" and "Back Door" Internet Connections

RB Enterprises recognizes that firewalls cannot protect against attacks that do not go through the firewall. It is concerned that a "helpful" employee might inadvertently end up giving modem pool access to an attacker. If and when that happens, the attacker will be able to break into the enterprise's network by completely bypassing the firewall and leak company proprietary data through that route.

RB Enterprises' management will ensure that Internet connections have a coherent policy about how dial-up access via modems should be protected. Management shall make the firewall a part of a consistent overall organizational security architecture and guard against the possibility of users independently establishing back door modem accounts which could put the enterprise at risk.[19]

Reporting Security Problems

RB Enterprises will facilitate training of its employees to ensure protection of its computer resources from hackers who deliberately penetrate various enterprise systems from the Internet to damage the systems and databases. All employees must adhere to the procedures enunciated in these training sessions.

The employees will address problems and report suspected misuse of their accounts or other misuse they may notice through the company's electronic mail address ("security"). If they feel an immediate need to establish direct personal contact with an appropriate authority, they may approach the system administrator who manages Internet security.

The system administrator shall post warnings about security breaches and also issue immediate solutions and software patches to problems as they are discovered. The system administrator will further investigate the suspicious activities and maintain a log of the investigation, actions, and findings.

If the system administrator decides it is necessary to examine files belonging to a user, he or she will advise other senior management as necessary to ensure that the individual rights are not violated, and that the facilities, services, and data for which the system administrator is responsible are protected.

Virus Awareness

A virus attack is not immediately evident in most organizational settings. RB Enterprises understands that the initial infection can go unseen for months and by the time the problem is identified, the damage may be widespread.

To prevent virus attacks, RB Enterprises shall maintain a strong and enforced company policy against any illegal software. The Enterprise systems administrator will keep the employees informed about the distinction between normal control structures and viruses, and set up controls to trap and eliminate computer viruses.

RB Enterprises is fully aware that viruses are brought in by contact with infected disks, or by local programming. Trojan Horses are crude, front door attacks, and they can be inadvertently introduced via a network, or on a disk. Accordingly, RB Enterprises mandates the system administrator to specifically address:

Risks of Download

The enterprise-level system administrator shall have the responsibility and authority to limit downloading of software packages from the Internet, if that is in the best interest of the company.

Additionally, to protect against downloading viruses, organizational-level system administrators will instruct all employees to perform virus check on all files downloaded. This policy also addresses files that are attachments to e-mail messages.

RB Enterprises employees shall:

1. Download files to a floppy disk and check for viruses before putting them on the computer's hard drive.
2. Perform a second check of the decompressed files if the originals are compressed files.

Problems of Virus Scanning

The system administrator will perform integrity checks, virus detection and removal, and immediately alert the company employees if any newer virus strains successfully penetrate virus scanning at the firewall or the desk top.

To establish further preventive security measures, the system administrator shall have the authority and responsibility to perform periodic checks for unacceptable use on those systems that allow remote access.

SUPPORT RESOURCES

As noted earlier, the proliferation of electronic bulletin boards combined with the growth of the Internet, allows RB Enterprises to place information on Web servers which can be easily and legally accessed by the consumers. To reiterate the steps outlined under the Effective and

Efficient Usage policy, RB Enterprises shall take great care to ensure that only properly reviewed and cleared information is placed on the Internet, inclusive of replies via electronic mail.

Who Authorizes Usage

In accordance with the policy stated under the subsection Web Pages Must Professionally Represent Enterprise, all RB Enterprises' web servers connected to the Internet must receive authorization and approval by the enterprise WebMaster and the respective organizational-level Web-Masters prior to being put into production. Failure to receive authorization will result in automatic disconnection from the Internet.

Who Maintains Web Presence

Refer to responsibilities addressed under subsection Web Pages Must Professionally Represent Enterprise.

DISCIPLINARY ACTIONS FOR POLICY VIOLATIONS

Supervisory and management personnel, and others with responsibility for Internet resources shall ensure that RB Enterprises' employees are informed of their responsibilities on the use of Internet. Employees are to avoid any use of the Internet services that violate the RB Enterprises' standards of conduct. Further, this directive states without any reservation that management will not tolerate prohibited uses of the Internet services on RB Enterprises resources, and violators will be subject to disciplinary action.

For disciplinary action, RB Enterprises will follow the approach endorsed by law enforcement and prosecutors. Under this approach, intruders will continue their activities at the site until the company apprehends the right person(s).

There is no global policy regarding the actual disciplinary action(s) to be taken. Such actions will be based on the severity of the damage, disruptions caused by the present and possibly future penetrations, attack frequency, financial or other risks to assets, and so forth.

HR managers shall ensure that all RB Enterprises' employees, especially those who are Internet users, know about the requirements set forth here.

Further, through periodic log-on messages, Enterprise WebMaster shall remind the Internet users of this requirement and their individual responsibilities under the law.

POLICY REVIEW COMMITTEE REPRESENTATIVES

Enterprise WebMaster, as stated under the subsection Web Pages Must Professionally Represent Enterprise, shall form a policy review committee with appropriate representation from the various RB Enterprises' organizations. These representatives will have the authority to speak for their respective business areas. The committee will serve to review, interpret, and revise this policy directive, as required.

APPENDIX: NETIQUETTE TUTORIAL

These are available from many vendors. Include the one that you feel is most comprehensive.

CORPORATE E-MAIL AND SECURITY POLICIES

Include these as attachments to this directive. If you don't have anything written on these issues, you need to develop additional guidelines.*

Conclusions

There are two main sources from which the problems arise: from hardware and software malfunctions and from misuse by human beings. With

---

* The author thanks Oliver Smoot of ITA, Walter Okon of DISA, Mark Gordon, Christopher Gallinari, Barry Weiss, and Diana McKenzie of Gordon and Glickson Law Offices for their encouragement and support in the creation of this example of Internet Policy Directive. While he is grateful for the exchange of ideas with and contributions of those mentioned above, final responsibility for the style, content, and views expressed herein rests with the author.

the widespread use of the Internet which has the capability to link everything to unknown strangers, many enterprises have become newly vulnerable to human misuse of Internet services in the form of hacking, the creation of viruses, invasions of privacy, and so on. The above statement of policy concerning the proper use of the resources of the Internet only partially covers all of the major problem areas. Each enterprise planning to issue an Internet policy must work out more details on the technical and organizational interface responsibilities: What does the HR do? How does it coordinate with the legal affairs and security?

APPENDIX B

Hardware and Software Issues

The author hopes that after reading this book, many of you will conclude that the Internet's extraordinary array of inexpensive global communication resources makes it an indispensable part of a contemporary enterprise. Yet many enterprises have little or no experience with Internet's technologies. Effective enterprise integration with the Internet and satellite systems requires a solid understanding of hardware and software solutions relative to connecting to the Internet, setting up an Internet server, assigning hostnames and IP numbers, providing TCP/IP services, and choosing a package of client software. This appendix is for those readers who are not conversant with the TCP/IP, Unix, or the Internet. For these readers, the best approach to Internet connectivity is to: (a) review and stock up on books that describe the various Internet connectivity options, and (b) initially contract with an outside provider who can offer a total Internet solution that includes connectivity via satellite systems that are being deployed globally.

The following reference books are recommended for understanding the hardware and software issues connected with the various configuration options. Each reference is annotated to identify and specify the chapters and sections germane to initial and more complex Internet setup and connectivity issues.

1. Daniel Minoli, *Internet and Intranet Engineering: Technologies, Protocols, and Applications*, McGraw-Hill, Inc., September 1996.

This primer on Internet technology, protocols, and applications is the first to baseline the Internet engineering effort and to define the parameters of the technical environment. It explains the contributing technologies of today's Internet in relatively brief and simple terms. It outlines new emerging directions, and surveys the technologies that will shortly create an environment quite different from today's "best effort" paradigm.

2. Kesahav S. Keshav, *An Engineering Approach to Computer Networking: ATM Networks, the Internet, and the Telephone Network*, Addison Wesley Longman, Inc., April 1997.

This book includes the very latest network technology covering protocol layering, multiple access, switching, scheduling, naming, addressing, routing, error and flow control, and traffic management. It also examines the pros and cons of several alternative solutions.

3. John R. Levine, Margaret Levine, and Young Carol Baroudi, *The Internet for Dummies*, IDG Books Worldwide, February 1999.

The *Internet For Dummies*, *4th Edition* is a beginner's reference on how to find information for hooking up with local Internet providers, including the hardware and software requirements that must be assessed. Chapters 2 and 21 will be of particular interest to the reader as they discuss the hardware/software identification process.

4. Frank J. Derfler and Les Freed, *How Networks Work, 4th Edition*, MCP SW Int., January 1998

This book discusses the fundamentals of connectivity including such topics as network operating system software, the logical topology that forms the heart of the local area network, ISDN lines, LAN, different types of network cables, and ATM switches. Of particular interest are Chapters 8–12, 14–22, 25, and 26 which provide detailed design information including specific hardware and software needs such as the RS-232C serial interface, smart modems, network operating systems, the network interface card, network cabling, server-based LANs, peer-to-peer networks, enterprise network systems, remote LAN access, network security, repeaters, bridges, routers, switches, packet-switching networks, and Internet connections.

5. Kevin Dowd and Mike Loukides (editor), *Getting Connected*, O'Reilly & Associates, Incorporated, January 1996

This book focuses on high-speed dedicated connections and draws from many different experiences in setting up Internet connections for business and for industry. It covers communications infrastructure; data link protocols including PPP, frame relay, X.25, HDLC, ATM, and SMDS; physical connection types including 56K leased lines, T1, T3, ISDN, and SONET; router configurations; Internet security including firewalls and proxy servers; configuration of DNS, mail, WWW, news, and FTP servers; and the extending of Internet services to desktop PCs and Macintoshes.

6. F. Andrew, *Connecting to the Internet: A Practical Guide about LAN-Internet Connectivity*, Addison Wesley Longman, Inc., February 1999.

This book discusses the entire process of connecting a private network to the Internet and maintaining that connection. This is a practical handbook that provides a step-by-step approach for planning, designing, implementing, and maintaining an effective and secure LAN-to-Internet connection —from TCP/IP essentials to choosing the most appropriate Internet Service Provider and setting up a firewall.

7. Bassam Halabi, *Internet Routing Architectures* (Cisco Press Development and Implementation Series), New Riders, April 1997.

This reference provides step-by-step instructions on how to construct and support robust ISP connections to the Internet. The book illustrates inter- and intra-domain routing issues, topologies, and scenarios for practical application.

8. Craig Hunt and Mike Loukides (editor), *Networking Personal Computers with TCP/IP*, O'Reilly & Associates, Incorporated, April 1995.

Most network administrators have the formidable task of integrating multisite, multiprotocol, heterogeneous networks, such as a TCP/IP-based network of UNIX systems (possibly connected to the Internet), a separate NetWare or NetBIOS network for the PCs, and even separate NetWare and NetBIOS networks in different departments or at different sites. This book gives practical information, as well as detailed instructions, for attaching PCs to a TCP/IP network, including basic TCP/IP configuration information for the most popular PC operating systems, and configuration of specific applications such as e-mail, remote printing, and file sharing. Installation of public domain TCP/IP software for the PC is described in an Appendix. Novell's NetWare, the most popular PC LAN software, is covered in a separate chapter.

9. Christian Huitema, *Routing in the Internet*, Prentice Hall, March 1995.

This book presents IP (the Internet Protocol); RIP (the most widely used "interior gateway"); EGP (the first "external gateway protocol"); BGP (the new "border gateway protocol"); and the recently developed CIDR (Classless Inter-Domain Routing). A separate chapter presents the requirements of "policy-based routing" and describes in detail the recent advances in routing technology including multicast transmission, mobile hosts, and the support of real time applications. These are technologies that will be used by the next generation of the Internet Protocol, IPv6, which will connect thousands of billions of hosts in the twenty-first century.

10. Douglas E. Comer, *The Internet Book: Everything You Need to Know about Computer Networking and How the Internet Works*, 2nd ed., Prentice Hall Press, January 1997.

The book provides practical guidance on Internet and networking technology, including basic communication, local area networks, packet switching, software for reliable communication, distributed computing, how the Internet works, software to create a virtual network, and why the Internet works well.

11. Galen A. Grimes and Rick Bolton, *10 Minute Guide to the Internet and World Wide Web*, 3rd ed., Macmillan Computer Publishing, January 1997.

This book describes the hardware and software needed to access the web; the use of Microsoft Internet Explorer, Netscape Navigator, and Netscape plug-ins; PointCast and Push Technology; configuration for Windows 95; and introduces several other important aspects of the technology.

Joint Ventures: Planning and Actions

Deal Issues

Alliances in telecommunications take many forms, including joint ventures, legal partnerships, and pure collaborations. While the main structural "drivers" behind these alliances remain fiscal,[1] the telecommunications environment has produced its own rules that impact the structure. Foreign ownership limitations, competition controls, and regulatory obligations have greatly impacted telecommunications trade and development activities in Africa, Asia, Latin America, and the Middle East.[2] All these factors have come under review in the context of the WTO and in the aftermath of the 1997 economic turmoil in the world. They have influenced the way partnerships in Africa and elsewhere are arranged and will continue to impact the way alliance/joint venture deals are struck and maintained.[3]

Contextually, partnerships could be for a specific country or for regional or global competitive activities.[4] Country-based cooperative agreements are complex, because not only must they operate in their home country, but also as facilitators in other related countries in a region.[5] Taiwanese and Hong Kong firms, for example, offer expertise to their Western partners as they expand into China. Similarly, South African entrepreneurs lend their support to the foreign partners as they expand into other parts of the continent. In global partnerships, partners combine their resources, assets, and competencies to improve their overall competitiveness in major global and regional markets; success or failure impacts the global competitive advantages of participating firms.[6–7]

In Africa, as in other countries throughout the world, partnerships have taken various legal forms. In general, agreements have regulated joint marketing activities and set up consortia. Frequently, agreements between Western and Asian or African or Latin American firms have established separate legal entities, or equity joint ventures, in which two or more partners have invested tangible and intangible capital. The joint venture company then concludes other contracts related to the use of brand names or transfer of technology under the umbrella of an overall partnership agreement encompassing licensing, management contract, franchising, and such with the individual partners.

The legal structure of an agreement indicates who is responsible for what, but does not necessarily clarify the distribution of power and control between the partners.[8] For the foreign partner in Asia, Africa, Latin America, and the Middle East, a 51 percent share in an equity joint venture and a majority on the board in an Asian, African, Latin American, or a Middle Eastern venture does not necessarily ensure that the partnership's activities are managed according to its wishes.[9] Alliances/joint ventures are influenced by pressures from the local government, by the partners, and by the managers who help create them.

That is the point of departure for this section, as it underscores the importance of developing a clear and sophisticated understanding of the environment where alliances/joint ventures operate. More specifically, it discusses the deals that must be negotiated, implemented, and managed in cooperative telecommunications ventures.[10]

THE OBJECTIVES OF THE PARTIES

In setting the framework around which major corporate commitments of long duration are to be made, the first priority should be to identify corporate objectives and their preparatory role.[11] Table C.1 provides observations on corporate objectives, as they relate to joint venture planning and action.

Table C.I Joint Venture Planning and Action

Preparations	Observations
Defining	A vital primary step in all corporate planning, no matter what action is selected.
Formulating simple or complex objectives	The foundation for all future plans and their implementation because they provide a basis for decision making and evaluating results.
	Management should define objectives that are valid for a maximum period of time.

Corporate management often engages in preliminary preparation of objectives through recognition of policies, preferences, and other internal and external influences. As these objectives are established, an analysis of the market extension, product extension, integration, technology transfer, diversification, and related strategies becomes important.[12] Table C.2 indicates how a fully orchestrated analysis can help provide the background for joint venture action.

FORM OF EQUITY

Whether global or national/regional/local players, firms often have strong views on what form their entry should take. Some companies may describe a penetration into a foreign country as a joint venture if a significant part (e.g., 20 to 30 percent) of the equity in the foreign operation is held by a local investor or investment group. This is not a joint venture, in the strict sense of the word. Rather, it is a simple minority investment by private (as opposed to public) shareholders. All policy, product and process know-how, and day-to-day administration of the business would necessarily flow from the parent, directly or through local nationals trained as any other new employee would be trained by the operating partner. The give-and-take of a true joint venture does not occur with a minority investment.[13]

There is no absolute definition of joint venture in terms of the percentage of equity that any one partner may hold, but for practical guidelines, inequality of equity should not exceed 60/40 percent for a two-party venture. Equity should be distributed more or less equally.[14]

Table C.2 Corporate Objectives and Strategy

Available Strategies	Observations
Market Extension	The firm may wish to participate in one or more foreign markets in a direct and integrated operation.
	It may sell to that market through normal export-import procedures or participate directly in a marketing operation in that market.
	Preemption by early entry prevents the competition from gaining a foothold.
	If joint venture is to be used, the partner can quickly penetrate foreign markets through market familiarity, organization, and, in some instances, particular processing skills.
	Market extension is the most widely used tactic in foreign markets in carrying out a corporate growth objective, and forms the basis for joint venture action.
Product Extension	Aggressive, profitable growth may sometimes be difficult, if not impossible, in existing product lines.
	Greater market share may not provide adequate return on incremental investment.
	If new markets (market extension) are precluded, the only growth alternative is to take on new products (product extension).
	New product development by one partner utilizing another partner's market position and skills is an ideal condition for joint venture.
Integration	This tactic consists of movement into a customer's business (forward integration) or into a supplier's business (backward integration).
	Integration through joint venture creates a new supplier or a new buyer.
Technology Transfer	Technology transfer, including business or commercial know-how as well as engineering or scientific transfer, has long been a basis for foreign joint ventures.
Diversification	Common definition is movement into new markets, usually to find new business areas that are countercyclical to the old business.
	Joint venture can be a successful method for diversification, provided each partner makes substantive contributions other than capital.
	Joint ventures begin and remain with a technology or product line. In foreign ventures, diversification may be the only effective way the parents can penetrate the markets of the host country.

Whatever the number of players, one equity partner must not dominate the business. In some instances, where one partner holds less than 50 percent of voting equity, it may be prudent to prepare an agreement so that voting controls, election of directors, and such, ensure equality to the otherwise minority holder. The distortion in agreements where this form of equality is expressed, and where less than 40 percent of equity is held by one of two partners, could generate frictions and inequities sufficient to make the relationship ultimately untenable.[15]

In contrast to a joint venture, a subsidiary is a corporation that is directly or indirectly controlled by another corporation. The usual condition of control is ownership of a majority (over 50 percent) of the outstanding voting stock. Table C.3 highlights the distinction.

Investment agreements with employees are not within the general spirit of joint venture. With the passage of time, these agreements may be viewed as a form of joint participation by the employees of the host country, as they become increasingly greater shareholders in the local venture. This form of ownership can provide certain tactical advantages in that there might be less governmental and populist negative reaction than would be created in a wholly owned foreign subsidiary.

TAX STRUCTURING

Salient tax-related points in structuring a joint venture need to be discussed in the proper context:[16]

- What are the tax benefits of an investment tax credit to the partnership form?

Table C.3 Contrast Between a Joint Venture and a Subsidiary

Organization	Controlling Authority
Joint Venture	The partners collectively control all areas essential to the accomplishment of the venture; none of the individual partners is in a position to unilaterally control the venture.
Subsidiary	Majority control and significant influence.

- Is tax payable on the transfer of partnership assets to the corporate co-owners upon liquidation?
- What are the tax implications upon termination of a venture?

For obvious advantages to the partnership form, these and other country-specific technical tax matters should be reviewed with competent tax counsel experienced in the particular country's legal framework.

INVESTMENT CONTRIBUTIONS

The deal should identify the estimated total investment amount required.[17]

BUSINESS PLAN AND FINANCING

A strategic alliance/joint venture has many problems to resolve. Its ultimate success depends largely on the skills devoted to the formation, negotiation, start-up, and attendant changes that occur through its inception. Common sense and general business acumen are necessary, but dependence on them alone is risky because strategic alliance/joint venture has built-in self-destruct devices. With or without business planning, some of the devices remain throughout the life of the alliance. For example, two or more partners bring two or more independent organizations into the position of having to share control. This requires constant reaffirmation of mutual respect. A signed document, namely the Formation Agreement to form a Joint Venture, will ensure such reaffirmation.

Specific issues for a joint venture with new products in a new market warrant immediate consideration.[18] Without adequate recognition and treatment of these issues in the formation stage and in agreements, seeds of destruction may be sown. Accordingly, the Formation Agreement should cover the objectives of the venture, management structure, action processes, capitalization and financing, and related subjects. Other agreements, such as an Operation Agreement, a Technology Transfer Agreement, and a Service Agreement, are attached to the Formation Agreement. These agreements ensure that all significant concepts or provisions, including business purpose, parties' intent, competitive considerations, the corporate opportunity, financing, and the obligation of all parties to make available to the alliance/joint venture any new technology, know-how, inventions, or software developed after the venture is formed, are clearly stated to avoid delays, frustrations, and eventual failure of the venture.[19]

Table C.4 identifies and comments on the elements that must be included in a business plan.

Table C.4 Business Plan and Approach

Elements	Contents
A written statement	• General business purpose • Operating policies • Objectives (with some tangible statements) • Goals of time • Product line • Geographic market applicable • Sales volume • Capital requirements • Reinvestment • Return on Investment, etc.
Justification	Why preference for alliance/joint venture as opposed to 100 percent ownership or minority position, including attitudes toward extrication.
Strengths and contributions that the initiating partner wants others to supply	These are the: • Missing attributes of the prime mover • Recognition of the impracticality of the initiator participating in a given market, or with given products, in view of lack of expertise or presence, as it is normally the case in a foreign country.
Composition and selection of the initial negotiating teams	Definition of the roles each is expected to fill.
Assets available	• Description of both tangible and intangible assets • Terms of transfer to the alliance/joint venture These provide a rough value of the equity of each partner.
Benefits	Advantages to each of the alliance partners.

Additionally, the business plan should indicate the initial paid-in capital and the value attributable to the know-how, patents, trademarks, and such, which are to be supplied by the alliance members. Further, it should articulate what other capital funds the new company may require, when they will be procured, the means of procuring the funds (e.g., loans), and the future obligations of the individual alliance members (e.g., secure loans in proportion to their ownership interests). The business plan should underscore that, if the facilities are to be expanded in the future, the financing will be accomplished so that the respective ownership interests remain unchanged.[20]

Careful treatment of these points will draw out the alliance partner commitments, which may be inherent in the joint venture. In view of the changing regulatory environment in Africa, tax implications, repatriation and foreign reinvestment of capital, and profits might influence the deal issues. These elements should receive consideration as the business plan, including the financing package, is assessed, identified, and prepared for final review and agreement.

FUTURE ACCESS TO CAPITAL

Financing for growth may present a major challenge to the continuity of an alliance/joint venture. For instance, one partner may wish to reinvest cash flows or even add new capital for strategic reasons, whereas the other partner(s) may be unwilling or unable to finance growth. The challenge is to accommodate all partners' objectives and changing circumstances, whenever possible.[21] Options available for future access to capital may include:

1. Varying the equity holding relationship and providing cash from one partner to the other.
2. Financing all or part of the growth through recapitalization, with preferred stock issued to outsiders or to the growth-oriented partner.
3. Debt financing, which may provide a lower cost of capital than any other mode.
4. A financial resource, such as a development bank sponsored by a host of foreign industrial countries.

Any requirements of alliance/joint venture partners for providing additional financing through debt, equity, or both must be spelled out. Terms such as dividend or interest rates, redemption rights, terms of loan, and such, should be considered in as much detail as possible if the financing is mandatory. Any limitation on outside financing should be included and cross-referenced to organizational papers.[22]

MANAGEMENT, PARTICULARLY VOTING CONTROL

Management considerations are part of the entire function of alliance/joint ventures. The major considerations include:[23-24]

1. Management: Board of Directors' representation and method of changing Directors. Also, composition of officers if other than by Directors' vote under state law.

2. Operational management: In an alliance structure, there are always multiple reporting and advisory relationships. One of the ways to offset this multiplicity is through the selection of activities for which each is responsible; the primary functions should always have clear reporting implications. The administration will find it productive to set up systems to report details to each alliance/joint venture partner so as to benefit from the dividend partners' responsibility and still control the business as a single entity.

3. Contact with partners: The alliance/joint venture must set up means of securing adequate contact with the partners to assure a constant flow of new technology or business techniques from the partners.

   Personal contact is the only way for the alliance/joint venture partners to maintain responsibility for the environment and problems faced by the venture. This is similar to the need in a geographically dispersed business, but it presents the unique challenge of reconciling the perspectives of two or more alliance/joint venture partners. It is compounded by two additional factors: (1) partners' different nationalities, and

(2) location of the alliance/joint venture in a different culture/economic environment.

At the time a strategic alliance/joint venture relationship is formed, an understanding must be reached concerning how the contact should be established and maintained, with budget and philosophy stipulations. Where responsibilities frequently change within the parent's operations, unexpected problems need to be minimized by keeping a readily identifiable "home office" contact.

4. Restrictions: In strategic alliance/joint venture deals, certain corporate actions should be taken only with the consent of all partners, thereby allowing each partner to review possible procedural or substantive actions that might adversely affect its investment. Restrictions, such as the veto power of each partner, may then be appropriately imposed on such actions in the corporate organization papers. This is particularly important for the partner with a minority interest in the venture. Table C.5 identifies the type of actions that should be reviewed.

After determining which corporate actions should be subject to veto, the procedure for establishing the veto power should be addressed. Restrictions may be included in the organization papers, thereby forcing an amendment process that would require stockholder approval and formal amendment papers. To amplify the point, each partner must vote its stock in the venture, and depending on the charter, by-laws, and such of the partner, the procedure for voting the stock might require approval by top management, and possibly even the board of directors.

If the restrictions are included in the Formation Agreement, which they usually are, they could be amended or modified by any authorized officer or by any partner having apparent authority. Such amendments need not be signed by top management, and, in fact, may not even need to be in writing, unless otherwise stated in the agreement. Thus, the inclusion of the restrictions in the organization papers would serve two purposes: (1) it would protect against an inadvertent waiver or modification of the restrictions, and (2) it would ensure top management scrutiny of any proposed change.

Table C.5 Procedural and Substantive Actions

Actions	Influences
Management	• Election or change of directors, or number of directors • Election or change in chief executive officer or other key officers
Business activities	• Change in business purpose clause • Termination of business, or part of it • Engaging in new business • Entering in any transaction or business arrangement with a co-owner or in which he or she has an interest
Organizational	• Reorganization • Merger, acquisition, consolidation, or other joint venture or other business combination • Recapitalization, reclassification, or change in terms of co-owners' stock (or other evidence of ownership) • Issue, sale, redemption, or purchase of the venture's stock or other securities • Change in charter, by-laws, or other organization documents • Liquidation or dissolution
Financial	• Incurrence of debt. Possibly there should be a limit on the amount the venture can borrow or on any financing outside of the ordinary course of business for other than working capital needs. • Capital expenditures in excess of ordinary needs of the business • Incurrence of contractual obligations with a risk factor in excess of a certain dollar amount • Transfer or pledges of a substantial part of the assets

INTELLECTUAL PROPERTY RIGHTS AND TECHNOLOGY TRANSFER

This provision can be a separate agreement, or simply a two-line provision, depending on the nature of the alliance/joint venture. If it is to provide services, with no software or intellectual property involved, the provision can be limited to making available know-how relevant to the services to be provided.

If the strategic alliance/joint venture involves a significant number of innovations in telecommunications equipment and trade secrets, with or without patent protection, the documentation involving intellectual property rights and technology transfer agreement should include licensing agreements with the concomitant consideration of exclusivity, geographical limitations, rights to improvements, royalties, and such. Further, the document should state the requirements for confidentiality and protection of trade secrets by appropriate safeguards.

The partners have other obligations. For example, the partners should make available to the alliance/joint venture any new technology, know-how, inventions, or software developed after the alliance is established. At the time of negotiating the deal, these matters should be discussed, together with the price, if the items are made available; for example, should any such item be provided at no cost, development cost, transfer cost, market value, or a combination of these?

It is crucial to settle these points in advance to avoid later misunderstandings.[25–26]

NON-COMPETE

The international telecommunications environment raises complex issues, because the participants include national telecommunications operators which are monopolies or former monopolies in their home countries. Most of them are teaming up with U.S. carriers and European operators to qualify themselves as global, nearly global, regional, and national champions that provide international one-stop services. In an African, Asian, Latin American, or Middle Eastern environment, the local parties to the alliance have already established their own businesses in the operation of networks, provision of services, or the supply of equipment. While negotiating the alliance structure, they need to understand that any discrimination in either direction, whether in favor of the parents or the venture, might risk infringement of competition rules, particularly where the parents or the venture itself have significant market share.

To date, members of most major alliances have been competing with each other in markets that are part of or closely related to the markets in which the alliance will be active. Eventually these alliances will raise insurmountable competition concern, except where they are aimed at combining the necessary resources, skills, and geographic coverage to enter newly emerging African, Asian, Latin American, or Middle Eastern markets strongly demanded by the business community. For example, there is a definite need to address the issue of where *not* to compete in order to obtain assurances guaranteeing open access to necessary facilities.[27] There should be an agreement that:

- Constrains the alliance/joint venture company from engaging in, either directly or indirectly, any business in the host country which is inimical to the joint venture.
- Directs the alliance/joint venture to ratify a technical supply or assistance agreement, thereby assuring the foreign partner of its arrangements with the alliance/joint venture as opposed to reliance on the agreements with the local host country partner(s).

EXIT POSSIBILITIES

Telecoms strategic alliances/joint ventures are conceived and started with every intention of becoming a permanent entity. However, circumstantial developments may necessitate that the investors liquidate their position. Therefore, the alliance/joint venture agreement should contain assurances that each partner will get the best possible value for its share if and when the need to pull out arises. The agreement should identify the means of ensuring best possible value, which could include:

- A sale of one partner's interest to the other partner
- A sale of the interest to the third party (private or public, passive or active)
- A sale of the entire joint venture to a third party
- Some form of total liquidation or dissolution

In each of the preceding situations, a number of complications could arise, depending on the nature of the alliance/joint venture, its location, and such.

- There may not be any available third party with characteristics that match the remaining partner's interests
- The retiring party may wish to retrieve the patents and proprietary rights that it may have contributed to the alliance/joint venture
- The host country regulations may have been granted earlier with the intention of securing long-term technology transfer and continuing the infusion of know-how by a non-national that wishes to extricate himself
- The inability or unwillingness of the other partner to take any steps that would lead to the dissolution of the alliance/joint venture
- The valuation of the shares and assets of the venture

Withdrawal often coincides with a period when the venture suffers from some problem, such as a decline in product/service demand or profitability or both, because of general economic turmoil in a given region. Equally likely, there may be a change in either partner's objectives or resources to make the venture incompatible with the partner's future programs. In the event these developments occur, the alliance/joint venture partners should be ready with possible terms, conditions, and methods of extrication to permit an orderly exit.[28–29] The varieties of possible extrication or termination procedures are endless and it is beyond the scope of this section to deal with them in detail. However, the following observations may offer guidelines for developing appropriate procedures:

- If future prospects are good, one party should not be able to buy (or force) the other out (except at a premium reflective of the future).
- If prospects are bleak, one party should not be able to force the other to take over (except at a discount reflective of the future).
- Either party should be able to force either extrication or termination with some penalty (but not so much as to be grossly unfair), in the event the alliance/joint venture is being run in a fashion inimical to that party's reputation or business interest.

- The incentive should be such as to encourage development of the business jointly, and to discourage extrication or termination.

If substitute partners are available, a frequently used mechanism is the right of first refusal and sale to an appropriate third-party purchaser. If one partner wants to get out, he can sell back to the other partner(s) of the alliance/joint venture. If none of them agree to a price, the partner wanting to extricate can obtain a firm offer from a third party, and other partners then have the right to purchase the shares on those offered terms. If the other partners do not exercise that right, the shares may be sold to the third party. The major disadvantage of this scheme is that a new partner can be forced onto the other partners, if they do not have the financial wherewithal, or are otherwise unable or unwilling to purchase the offered shares.

DISPUTE RESOLUTION

While negotiating an alliance/joint venture, there should be clear consensus as to how disputes with respect to the agreement are to be settled.[30]

Conflict Issues

WHY DO SO MANY ALLIANCES FAIL?

While discussing the form of equity, the alliance/joint venture was described as resulting from agreements between or among multiple partners. Under any given agreement, one partner could have less than 50 percent of voting equity, but it must be carefully drafted and presented to cover voting controls, election of directors, and such so as to ensure equality to the otherwise minority holder. Wherever this form of equality is expressed, and less than 40 percent of equity is held by one of two partners, any distortion in agreements would likely generate frictions and inequities sufficient to make the relationship ultimately untenable.[31]

An alliance/joint venture, as discussed here, differs from other business arrangements in that all areas essential to the accomplishment of the venture are collectively controlled by the alliance/joint venture partners. None of the individual partners is in a position to unilaterally control the venture. This feature of joint control is substantially different from majority control (e.g., subsidiary) and significant influence.

An ideal situation in an alliance/joint venture is where one side is willing to administer the local content and have day-to-day operational responsibility, and the other supplies technical know-how, including formulations and customer applications. In actual cases, however, there could be multiple partners with no one in control, a situation that creates problems.

The requisites for managing the ventures and protecting the partners' interests are to spell out the alliance/joint venture policies and operations by agreements in writing. These agreements become the basis for assessing and adjudicating issues for the alliance/joint venture. This must be understood and stressed in implementation. In the same vein, a clear-cut statement that the operation of a given venture over a long period of time will also get the benefit of top management attention is something that should be expressed and abided by in practice. As the alliance/joint venture continues, issues will surface to challenge the alliance partners' policies. If top management is not prepared to address these issues effectively, comprehensively, and decisively, delays in decisions will inevitably occur, raising questions about the efficiency and viability of the alliance/joint venture.

Another issue that could jeopardize an alliance structure is the conflict of reinvestment for growth versus dividend return.[32] One partner may have resources to reinvest for the maximization of growth opportunity in a given market, but the other partner(s) may require net cash flow and dividend return. Following the recent economic downturn in certain parts of the world, this concern has been raised by the local partners in different regions' joint ventures. This is a very important issue and it must be placed on the agenda for early concurrence, paying full attention to the optimistic and pessimistic estimates on future investment needs, including responses to "what-if?" questions. Answers to these questions will provide measures of risk and financial exposure that might result, and will draw out the commitments that may be inherent in the project. In today's global environment, there is also a specific need for more current, more up-to-date financial studies on tax implications, repatriation, and reinvestment of capital and profits. Without adequate recognition and the treatment of these issues in the formation stage and in the agreement, seeds of destruction of the alliances/joint ventures are sown, where future failures are reaped.

Acronyms and Abbreviations

Address (network address)—Internet site addresses come in two forms: (1) as a set of 32 bit numbers, commonly expressed as a sequence of four decimal numbers such as 192.168.0.1; and (2) as alphanumerics such as mail.tpp.com. These can represent the same address, and either could be used, for example, with Telnet. People find the alphanumerics easier to remember than numbers. My own e-mail address at this site would be noted as amaitra@mail.tpp.com.

Anchor—A marker for the beginning or the end of a hypertext link.

Anonymous FTP—Accessing data via the File Transfer Protocol, or FTP, using the special user name "anonymous." This method provides restricted access to public data.

Archie—A service used to search thousands of FTP sites for any directory name, filename, string of characters, or words that users specify.

ARPANET (Advanced Research Projects Agency Network)—The granddaddy of the Internet. It was the original communications network created by the Advanced Research Projects Agency, a branch of the United States Department of Defense. It was designed to withstand any unforeseen events and give America the edge in any conflict.

ASCII (American Standard Code for Information Interchange)—A worldwide standard in which the numbers, uppercase letters, lowercase letters, some punctuation marks, some symbols, and some control codes have been assigned numbers from zero to 127. For instance, when using ASCII, the letter "a" is always stored as binary number 1000001. Documents created using only the ASCII characters are very easy to transfer over the Internet.

Authoring Tool—A program that partially automates the process of writing HTML.

Backbone—Refers to a high-speed network that links mid-level networks. It is used to expedite data passage from source to destination, where data are stored on computers or servers in various locations around the globe.

BBS (Bulletin Board System)—A remote computer user interface offering a way to post public messages in various topical discussion groups, receive files from and send files to the public, and access other remote computers and services via the Internet and/or through direct dial-up.

Binary—Refers to any data stored or transferred in digital form.

BITNET—An acronym for "Because It's Time Network." It is a global academic and research network started in 1981 and operated by EDUCOM.

Body—Refers to the main text or content of an HTML document.

Bounce—If an e-mail is undelivered, it is sent back (bounced) to the sender so that she or he will know the mail was not delivered.

Browser—A web client program (e.g., Microsoft Internet Explorer, Netscape) that sends requests for resources across networks and displays those resources when they are received.

Button—A graphical representation of a button on an area of a screen that is designed to be "clicked on" or otherwise selected for user input.

Campuswide Information System (CWIS)—A tool used for navigation and information retrieval. It provides data from a variety of campus sources available through one user interface.

CERN—The European Laboratory for Particle Physics in Geneva, Switzerland, where the web was first developed. The acronym CERN comes from the earlier French title: "Conseil European pour la Recherche Nucleaire."

Client/Server—Refers to information distribution on a network using a small number of server programs to provide data to client programs installed on many computers throughout the network. The database is maintained by the server program and, if and when requested by client programs, the server program retrieves information from the database and sends the information through the network to the client programs. The client programs offer a user-friendly and consistent interface.

Communications Software—Refers to programs running on a personal computer that allow the computer to communicate with a modem, and thus through the phone lines.

Cracker—A person using computer knowledge to attempt access to computer systems with the intention of maliciously damaging those systems and/or data in them.

Dial-in (also Dial-up)—Connection between two computers over standard voice grade telephone lines, usually via modems.

Discussion List—This is similar in some ways to a mailing list. The major difference is that the mailing list is sent to subscribers in one batch, whereas a discussion list forwards messages one at a time.

Domain Name—A group of names listed with dots (.) between them. This is an Internet addressing system. Inter-Networking Information Center (InterNIC) of Network Solutions, Inc. assigns and keeps track of all domain names in the United States where the most general domains are network categories such as edu (education), com (commercial), and gov (government). Countries use two-letter abbreviations such as ca (Canada), au (Australia), ch (Switzerland), de (Germany), it (Italy), nz (New Zealand), and sg (Singapore).

Download—To copy data from a remote computer to a local computer. The opposite is upload.

E-mail—A system used by computer users to exchange messages with other computer users (or a group of users) via a communications network. E-mail is the basis for discussion groups and many other Internet/intranet services.

E-zine—Refers to electronic magazines. These are the ultimate in do-it-yourself publishing.

FAQs (Frequently Asked Questions)—Newcomers arrive at Usenet newsgroups or e-mail lists all the time and want to find out the facts and guidelines about a particular topic and group. To respond to these newcomers, a document in question-and-answer format is assembled. These FAQs are revised at regular intervals to offer the most up-to-date information on a given subject.

Finger—An Internet system that allows the user to find out the name of a person who has an e-mail address, when the person last checked for mail, and several other items.

Freeware—Totally free software made available from many locations on the Internet (often via FTP).

FTP (File Transfer Protocol)—A protocol allowing a user on a host to access and transfer files to and from another host over the Internet.

Gateway—A computer that connects two or more networks, often to pass data between incompatible network systems.

GIF (Graphics Interchange Format)—CompuServe developed a type of picture storage file, now widely used on the Internet. Files in this format are designated by an extension of .gif.

Gopher—A widely used, menu-based storage system for files and links to other Internet resources. See Chapter 1.

Host—Internet access provider's computer.

HTML—Hypertext Markup Language used for world wide web documents.

HTTP—Hypertext Transfer Protocol. This is the Internet protocol that allows web clients to retrieve information from web servers.

Hypertext—Links information in a document to related information by address codes operating behind the scenes. A user simply clicks on highlighted text to call up more details on a topic or jump to a related topic—within one document or between documents. "Between documents" could mean anywhere on the world wide web (WWW).

Hytelnet—Frequently updated database, providing information about specific Telnet sites and aiding in the connection to them.

Internet—A digital communications network connecting various other (smaller) networks from around the world. Started in the United States, it transfers data using a standardized protocol called TCP/IP.

Intranet—Refers to the use of the Internet technologies within the enterprise to enhance user productivity.

IRC (Internet Relay Chat)—A popular method used on the Internet in order to find quick answers in real time to questions on a variety of topics. This method does not have as far a reach as posting to a newsgroup.

Listserv—An automated program that accepts mail messages from users and does basic operations on mailing lists (discussion groups) for those users. Listserv answers requests for indexes, FAQs, archives of the previous discussions, and other files.

Login—Used interchangeably with "logon." Refers to a process where a user wants to establish a connection to another computer. The process involves some user steps, such as entering a specific login password.

Logoff—To leave or disconnect from a computer system. Often accomplished by selecting a menu item for disconnecting.

Mailing List—A list of e-mail addresses used to discuss a certain set of topics. Different mailing lists discuss different topics. In the Internet, for those mailing lists maintained by a human rather than by a listserv, one can generally subscribe to a list by sending a mail message to "listname-REQUEST@host" and entering a request to subscribe in the body of the message. To send messages to other subscribers, one needs to use the address "listname@host."

Majordomo—Refers to a mail server software.

MODEM (Modulator/DEModulator)—An electronic device that converts the digital signals used by computers into analog signals needed by voice telephone systems. Virtually all modems combine the send and receive functions in one circuit.

Moderator—The moderators in various discussion groups watch the postings to ensure that the language and nature of the messages are suitable for public postings and that those postings relate to the overall topics and goals of the list.

Mosaic—A browser with a graphical user interface that enables users to forego standard text in place of graphics and sound. It is a public domain package, available free of charge from the National Center for Supercomputing Applications' (NCSA) Internet server.

Netscape (TM)—Refers to Netscape Communications Corporation's client software for enterprise networks and the Internet.

Network—Computers connected to facilitate data transmission among them. See Chapter 1.

Network Access Provider (Network Service Provider)—Any organization that provides network connectivity or dial-up access.

NIC (Network Information Center)—A central place that maintains information about a network within the Internet. Most network service providers also provide an NIC for their users.

Node—Refers to a computer that is directly connected to a network and is used to transfer and route data or provide end-user services.

NSFNET (National Science Foundation Network)—The system that the National Science Foundation, a U.S. government agency, created for high-speed data transfer links and nodes. It initially formed the backbone of the Internet.

Online—Refers to activity being carried out while a computer is connected to another computer or network.

PPP (Point to Point Protocol)—Refers to TCP/IP connections that use serial lines such as dial-up telephone lines. Similar to SLIP (see below), but it is a later standard that offers features such as compression, better flow control, etc.

Protocol—Represents a formal description of message formats involving timing, error control, etc., and a set of operating rules of data transmissions and other activities on a network.

Real Time—Describes particular moments when two or more people are communicating via computers at the same instant.

RFC (Requests For Comments)—The document series begun in 1969 that describes the Internet systems, protocols, proposals, etc.

Shareware—Software, initially available free, with authors expecting voluntary payments after an initial test period. There are functional limitations in the initial versions, with the promise of an upgrade available if the fee is paid. Usually reasonable prices.

SLIP (Serial Line Internet Protocol)—Refers to TCP/IP connections that use serial lines such as dial-up telephone lines. This is generally used at sites with few users as a less expensive alternative than a full Internet connection. SLIP is being replaced by PPP at many sites.

TCP/IP (Transmission Control Protocol/Internet Protocol)—Represents two major communications protocols used within the Internet: TCP and IP. These, together with several others, form the foundation for communications between hosts in the Internet. The various service protocols, such as FTP, Telnet, etc., use TCP/IP to transfer information.

Telnet—This Internet standard protocol is for remote terminal connection service.

Upload—Refers to copying data from a local computer to a remote computer. The opposite is download.

URL (Uniform Resource Locator)—Refers to the addressing scheme for resources on the web.

USENET Newsgroups—Like Listservs and mailing lists, these serve as forums for discussion on any given topic of interest. Messages posted to USENET usually are echoed to servers across the globe, allowing businesses to keep current with related corporate news and products, while broadening their exposure to thousands and even millions of Internet users.

User Name—Either assigned by an Internet Service Provider (ISP) or selected by an individual user, this represents a short name unique to a user on his or her ISP's system. This name, followed by an individual's site address, becomes the user's e-mail address.

UUCP (Unix to Unix Copy Program)—This was initially a protocol for communicating between consenting Unix systems via dial-up phone lines. The term is more commonly used today to describe a large international network that uses the UUCP protocol to pass news and electronic mail.

Veronica—Refers to a method used for searching available Gopher sites for information on a specific topic.

Virtual Reality—Refers to combinations of user-interface involving three-dimensional graphics, speech synthesis, speech recognition, and other features that closely mimic humans' normal operating experiences in the real world.

WAIS (Wide Area Information Service)—Refers to an indexing mechanism for larger databases.

WWW (world wide web or the web)—Refers to the hypertext-based, distributed information system created by researchers at CERN in Switzerland. The WWW servers are interconnected to allow a user to traverse the web from any starting point.

Notes

Chapter 1   Making the Internet Work

1. Amit K. Maitra, *Building a Corporate Internet Strategy: The IT Manager's Guide*, Van Nostrand Reinhold, August 1996.
2. Richard G. Mathieu, "Manufacturing and The Internet," Engineering and Management Press, 1998.

Chapter 2   Two Themes of Satellite-Based Internet Use

1. Project Management Advantages of the Internet, Semaphone Interactive, http://www.sema4.com/sema4/services/si/mansimp.htm
2. The Advantages of Team-based Project Management, A Netmosphere Whitepaper, http://www.netmosphere.com/actionplan/whitepapers/index.html
3. Netmosphere Project Home Page, http://www.netmosphere.com/projecthomepage/index.html
4. Netmosphere Action Plan, http://www.netmosphere.com/actionplan/index.html
5. Netmosphere Action Plan, http://www.netmosphere.com/actionplan/online-demo/screen02.html
6. Netmosphere Action Plan, http://www.netmosphere.com/actionplan/online-demo/screen03.html
7. Netmosphere Action Plan, http://www.netmosphere.com/actionplan/online-demo/screen09.html
8. Jack Rickard, "A Cache and Carry Internet," *Boardwatch*, February 1998.
9. Randy Barrett, "Caching Onto Satellite Services," *Inter@ctive Week*, 2 March 1998, p. 30.
10. Todd Spangler, "Promising Satellite Services Emerge as..." *Internet World*, 9 March 1998, p. 45.
11. Andy Eddy, "Satellite Net Access System Flush with...," *Network World*, 9 March 1998, p. 39.
12. Chris Oakes, "Can Caching Tame the Web," *Wired News*, 19 March 1998.
13. Mark Ribbing, "Making a Bid to Cache In on Internet," *The Baltimore Sun*, 19 March 1998, p. C1.

Chapter 3   Manufacturing and the Internet

1. Adedeji Bodunde Badiru, *Project Management in Manufacturing and High Technology Operations*, John Wiley & Sons, Inc., New York, 1996.

2. Adedeji Bodunde Badiru, *Managing Industrial Development Projects*, Van Nostrand Reinhold, New York, 1993.

3. Amit K. Maitra, *op. cit.*, pp. 34–38.

4. Sidney Hill Jr., "Running an Intelligent Enterprise," *Manufacturing Systems Special Reports*, October 1998, http://www.manufacturingsystems.com

5. Marty Weil, "The Enterprise Extended," *Manufacturing Systems Special Reports*, March 1998, http://www.manufacturingsystems.com/supplement/IBM2.htm

6. Marty Weil, "More Important Than Ever," *ManufacturingSystems Special Reports*, October 1998, http://www.manufacturingsystems.com

7. Jim Fulcher, "A Stable Mix—Successful ERP/MES Implementation Relies on Project Planning, Clear Goals," *Manufacturing Systems Special Reports*, May 1998, http://www.manufacturingsystems.com/supplement/ERP2.htm

8. A Reader's Guide to Next Generation EPR, *ManufacturingSystems Special Reports*, October 1997, http://www.manufacturingsystems.com/supplement/ERPlist.htm

9. Make Process Information Accessible Over Your Intranet, *Web@aGlance*, Intuitive Technology, http://www.aglance.com/newsite/newfeel/web_blurb.htm

10. Accessing Data with the Internet, http://www.software.rockwell.com/support/download/index.cfm

11. ActiveX Activates the Internet, http://www.microsoft.com

12. Heading Toward a Future of OLE Automation, http://www.microsoft.com

13. The Role of OPC, http://www.microsoft.com

14. Blazing New Trails on the Web, http://www.microsoft.com

Chapter 4   Satellite Internet Applications: Project Management Using ICO Global Communications Services

1. Thomas Caldwell, "The Sky's the Limit for Internet Access," http://www.cjmag.co.jp/magazine/issues/1998/june98/caldwell.html

2. Tom Wilson, "Aquarius Wired: Voice and Data Communication Over Satellite-Based Internet...," *Distant Star*, August 1998, http://www.distant-star.com/issue8/aug_98_feat_aquarius_wired.htm

3. Dr. Fulvio Ananasso, "Satellites and Information Superhighways: Quickly Deploying Global Communication Infrastructures," paper presented at the nineteenth annual Pacific Telecommunications Conference in Honolulu, Hawaii, January 1997.

4. Integrated Space/Terrestrial Mobile Networks, Action Final Summary, Cost 227, 1995, http://www.estec.esa.nl/xewww/cost227/summary.txt

5. Sayed Ali, Preetham Peter, and Jin White, "Digital Satellite Systems for Internet Access," http://fiddle.ee.vt.edu/courses/ee4984/Projects1997/ali_peter_white.html

6. Daniel Kohn, "The Teledesic Network: Using Low-Earth-Orbit Satellites to Provide Broadband, Wireless, Real-Time Internet Access Worldwide," http://www.iif.hu/inet_96/gl/gl_3.htm

7. Narrowband in the Era of Broadband, Communications Industry Researchers, Inc., 1998, http://www.cir-inc.com/reports/nb2/

8. Gary L. Garriott, "Low Earth Orbiting Satellites and Internet-Based Messaging Services," http://www.iif.hu/inet_96/gl/gl_1.htm

9. Mike B. Chivhanga, "The Potential for the Internet in Africa," a discussion between Dr. Tanya Bowyer-Bower of the School of Oriental and African Studies (SOAS) and Mike B. Chivhanga of Image Productions, 27 November 1997, http://virtual.finland.fi/kyo/english/chivhang.html

10. Jean-Yves Djamen, Dunia Ramazani, and Stephene Soteg Some, "Networking in Africa: An Unavoidable Evolution Towards the Internet," http://www.unisa.ac.za/dept/press/comca/212/djamen.html

11. Mike Jensen, "Bridging the Gaps in Internet Development in Africa," IDRC Study, 31 August 1996, http://www.idrc.ca/acacia/studies/ir-gaps5.htm

12. Pierre Dandjinou and Raul Zambrano, "Networking in Africa: UNDP's Sustainable Development Networking Program (SNDP): A Progress Report, February 1997, http://www.ghana.com/isoc/ans97/raul.htm

13. Michiel Hegener, "Telecommunications in Africa—Via Internet in Particular," http://155.135.37.1/fac/1press/devnat/general/africa.htm

14. Gary L. Garriot, *op. cit.*

15. Dr. Fulvio Ananasso, *op. cit.*

16. Lloyd Wood, "Big LEO Tables," L.Wood@surrey.ac.uk

17. Integrated Space/Terrestrial Mobile Networks, Action Final Summary, Cost 227, 1995, *op. cit.*

18. "The World's Phone," ICO-The Global Communications Magazine, Issue 1, Spring 1997.

19. Ibid.

20. ICO Corporate Profile, ICO Global Communications Inc., 21 April 1998.

21. System Description, ICO Satellite Constellation, ICO Global Communications Inc., April 1997.

22. ICO Corporate Profile, *op. cit.*

23. Anthony Brooks and Lawrence Edwards, "The South African Internet: First World vs. Third World," http://www.ghana.com/isoc/ans97/brooks.htm

24. "The World's Phone," *op. cit.*

25. "The Internet and Rural Development: Recommendation for Strategy and Activity," Chapter 3. Recommended FAO Strategy and Activity, 26 September 1996, http://www.fao.org/waicent/faoinfo/sustdev/CDdirect/CDDO/chapter3.htm

26. Niall Murphy and Daniel Erasmus, "A Model for Establishment of an Internet Infrastructure within the African Context, Case Study: Zimbabwe Internet Business Plan," presented at INET97—African Network Symposium, June 1997, http://www.ghana.com/isoc/ans97/niall.htm

27. "The World's Phone," *op. cit.*

28. Wendy White, "International Assistance for Internet Growth in Sub-Saharan Africa, ASIS Bulletin, June/July 1998, http://www.asis.org/Bulletin/Jun-98/white.html

29. Gary L. Garriott, *op. cit.*

30. Michiel Hegener, *op. cit.*

31. "The World's Phone," *op. cit.*

Chapter 5   Internet Caching

1. Web Caching: An Introduction, http://www.cs.ubc.ca/spider/mjmccut/webcache.html

2. Adrian Cockcroft, "Increase System Performance by Maximizing Your Cache," *Sunworld*, February 1997, http://www.sunworld.com/swol-02-1997/swol-02-perf.html

3. Karen Kaplan, "Future Internet Will Be Faster, More Versatile," *Los Angeles*, August 17, 1998, http://www.latimes.com/HOME/NEWS/CUTTING/lat_inet0817.htm

4. Robert E. Lee, "Caching to Relieve Bandwidth Congestion," *Sunworld*, June 1998, http://www.sunworld.com/swol-06-1998/swol-06-caching.html

5. B. Danzig, K. Worrell, M. Schwartz, A. Chankhunthod, and C. Neerdaels, "A Hierarchical Internet Object Cache," Technical Report CU-CS-766-95, University of Colorado, Boulder,

March 1995, as referenced in Margaret Dumont, Seminar Paper Survey of Worldwide Caching, University of British Columbia, http://www.cs.ubc.ca/spider/dumont/caching/caching.html

6. Kate Gerwig and Chuck Moozakis, "ISPs Gain New Weapons For Service Portfolios," *Internet Week*, October 5, 1998, Issue: 735, Section: News and Analysis, http://www.techweb.com/se/directlink.cgi?INW 19981005S0023

7. Barbara Darrow, "SkyCache Seeks to Break Web LogJam," *Computer ResellerNews*, August 3, 1998, Issue: 801, Section: News, http://www.techweb.com/se/directlink.cgi?CRN19980803S0003

8. "Renovating the Internet," SkyCache White Paper, SkyCache, February 5, 1998, http://www.skycache.com/products/index.html

9. Todd Spangler, "Promising Satellite Services Emerge As Alternative to Earthbound Lines," *Internet World*, 9 March 1998.

10. Jan Stafford, "Catch On To Web Caching—VARs and ISPs reap opportunities from a promising new market," *VAR Business*, October 26, 1998, Issue: 1422, Section: Technology – Hardware, http://www.techweb.com/se/directlink.cgi?VAR19981026S0028

11. "Why This Cache Is Just As Good As the Real Thing," 1998 Innovations, Planet Internet.

12. "Welcome To The InterCache Cache System WebSite!," 1998 InterCache LLC.

13. Denise Culver, "For Many Internet Providers, Cache Isn't King," *Inter@ctive Week*, October 5, 1998, http://www.zdnet.com/intweek/print/981005/357736.htm

14. David W. Crawford, "Pricing Network Usage: A Market for Bandwidth or Market for Communication," presented at MIT Workshop on Internet Economics, March 1995, http://www.press.umich.edu/jep/works/CrawMarket.html

15. Jon Knight and Martin Hamilton, "Caching in On Caching," http://www.ariadne.ac.uk/issue4/caching

16. J. Gwertzman and M. Seltzer, "The Case of Geographical Push-Caching," Proceedings of the 5th Annual Workshop on Hot Operating Systems, Orkas Island, WA, May 1995, pp. 51–55, As referenced in http://www.cs.ubc.ca/spider/dumont/caching/caching.html

17. Duane Wessels and K.C. Claffy, "A Distributed Architecture for Global WWW Cache Integration," Annual Progress Report March 15, 1997-March 14, 1998, http://ircache.nlanr.net/Cache/Reports/report.199803.html

18. Web Caching As a Viable Exchange Point Service, http://ircache.nlanr.net/Cache/mae-west

19. Ingrid Melve, "Caching Our Desire: Plan for Web Caching Activities," February 1997, http://www.uninett.no/prosjekt/desire/plan.html

20. Andre De Jong, Ton Verschuren, Henry Bekker, and Ingrid Melve, "Report on the Costs and Benefits of Operating Caching Services," http://www.surfnetnl/surfnet/projects/desire/deliver/WP4/D4-2.html

21. Michael Sparks, "Report on a Statistical Analysis of the National Cache Performance," November 1998, http://workshop@wwwcache.ja.net/Statistics/November_Graphs/Report.html

22. Andre De Jong et al., *op. cit.*

23. Ingrid Melve, *op. cit.*

24. Steven Glassman "A Caching Relay for the World Wide Web," System Research Center, Digital Equipment Corporation, Palo Alto, CA, steveg@pa.dec.com

25. Vicki Johnson and Marjory Johnson, "IP Multicast Backgrounder: An IP Multicast Initiative White Paper," Stardust Forums, Inc., http://www.ipmulticast.com/community/whitepapers/backgrounder.html

26. B. Quinn, "IP Multicast Applications: Challenges and Solutions," Internet Draft, November 1998, IP Multicast Initiative, Stardust Forums, Inc., http://www.ipmulticast.com/techcentral/draft-quinn-multicast-apps-00.txt

27. Salvatore Saloamone, "Satellite Web Service Improves International Access," *InternetWeek*, August 3, 1998, Issue 726, Section: News & Analysis, http://www.techweb.com/se/directlink.cgi?INW19980803S0015

28. "INTELSAT Awards Contract For Multicast Internet Caching and Replication System," INTELSAT News Releases, Washington, D.C., 9 February 1998.

29. "INTELSAT Multicasting Partners," INTELSAT News Releases, Washington, D.C., 18 August 1998.

Chapter 6   Managing Electric Utilities

1. Leslie Lamarre, "At Home With Telecommunications," *EPRI Journal*, January-February 1997, http://www.EPRI.com/epri_Journal/jan_feb97/telecom.html

2. Taylor Moore, "Tighter Security for Electronic Information," EPRI Journal, November December 1996, http://www.EPRI.com/epri_Journal/nov_dec96/secure.html

3. Internet Information Services: Home Energy Audit, Energy Interactive Inc., http://www.energyinteractive.com/web.audit.html

4. Trueblood, Nathan and John Powers, "Internet Information Services: Providing Content for Utility Customers," presented on behalf of Quantum Consulting, 1997–1998, http://energyinteractive.com/iqpc_nash_present/iqpc.01.html

5. Rich Lysakowski, "Use of the Internet for RD Team Computing Industry and Research Directions, http://www.lib.uchicago.edu/~atbrooks/CINF/abstract.html

6. Utility Industry—A Time of Transformation in the utility industry, http://www.utilities_industry.hosting.ibm.com/transf.htm

7. IRIS Project Status Report S96, http://wwwics.uci.edu/~rlamb/irisrpt5.html

8. CPUC Electric Restructuring-Procedural History, http://converger.com/California/CPUC%20ERP%20history.htm

9. The Future Energy Utility Company-Executive Summary, http://www.ftenergy.com/power/powrs13.htm

10. Ibid.

Chapter 7   Taking New Measures

1. Paul Strassmann, "40 Years of IT History," Datamation, 40th Anniversary Special Issue, October 1997.

2. Paul Strassmann, "The Value of Knowledge Capital," American Programmer, March, 1998.

3. Paul Strassmann, Private Briefing to the Federal Reserve Board, April 15, 1999, http://www.strassmann.com/index.html

4. Paul Strassmann, "What's the Key to Implementing Knowledge Management?," Interview, Knowledge Management Magazine, April 1999.

5. Paul Strassmann, "Beat The Clock," GCN, September 21, 1998.

6. Paul Strassmann, "What is Alignment?," Cutter IT Journal, August, 1998.

7. Paul Strassmann, "Of Men and Machines: Productivity Declines," Forbes, June 11, 1998.

8. Paul Strassmann, "Outsourcing IT: Miracle Cure or Emetic?," May, 1998, http://www.strassmann.com/index.html

9. Facts and Fantasies about Information Productivity, book excerpt CIO Hall of Fame, CIO Magazine, September 1997.

10. Strassmann on Politics and Guidelines, Review by Michael Schrage, Harvard Business Review, Sept-Oct, 1997.

11. Align for the Bottom Line, Review by Megan Santosus, CIO Magazine, August 1997.

12. Paul Strassmann, "Taking Computers To Task," Scientific American, July 1997.

13. Do U.S. Firms Spend Too Much on Information Technology?, Interview with Norm Alster, Investor's Business Daily, April 3, 1997.

14. Paul Strassmann, "Will Big Spending on Computers Guarantee Profitability?," Datamation, February 1997.

15. Paul Strassmann, "Has Business Squandered The IT Payoff?," Computer Finance, January 1997.

16. Paul Strassmann, *Information Productivity: Assessing the Information Management Costs of U.S. Industrial Corporations*, The Information Economics Press, 1999.

Appendix A   Internet Policy for the Enterprise

1. "FOCUS: Internet Policies," *WORK FORCE STRATEGIES—A Supplement to BNA's Employee Relations Weekly*, Volume 13, Number 33, August 21, 1995.

2. "Developing an Enterprise Internet Policy," Research Notes, Gartner Group, February 1995.

3. "Many Report Financial Losses and Internet Break-ins Due to Lax Computer Security," *PR Newswire* via Individual, Nov. 21, 1995.

4. Walter Okon, "WWW Structure for DISA's Web," A *White Paper, DISA*, September, 1995.

5. "U.S. Judge Rules Internet Services May be Liable for Postings," *Los Angeles Times*, November 29, 1995.

6. "Developing an Enterprise Internet Policy," Research Notes, Gartner Group, March 1995.

7. M. Gibbs, "An Acceptable Use Policy Can Derail Internet Distractions," *Network World*, September 26, 1995.

8. Cliff High of Tenax Software Engineering in Olympia, Washington was qouted in "FOCUS: Internet Policies," *WORKFORCE STRATEGIES—A Supplement To BNA's Employee Relations Weekly*, Volume 13, Number 33, August 21, 1995.

9. Yvonne Chiu, "E-Mail Gives Rise to the E-Wall—A Blizzard of Personal Chat Raises Worries About Office Productivity," *The Washington Post*, August 18, 1995.

10. Mark L. Gordon and Christopher L. Gallinari, "Don't Carry Nothin' Someone Else Has Sold: Ease On Down The Electronic Road," A review article by Gordon and Glickson P.C., Chicago, IL, 1995.

11. Diana J.P. McKenzie, "How To Minimize The Legal Costs of Doing Business On The Information Superhighway," A review article by Gordon and Glickson P.C., Chicago, IL, 1995.

12. Barry D. Weiss, "Implementing Sound Corporate Internet Policies: Legal and Management Issues," A review article by Gordon and Glickson P.C., Chicago, IL, 1995.

13. Michael Strangelove, "The Walls Come Down," *Internet World*, May 1995, p. 42, referenced in Barry D. Weiss, *op. cit.*, p. 17.

14. Bob Grzesik, "Psychotic E-Mail Can Make You Look Loonier Than You Are," Opinions in *INFOWORLD*, Volume 17, Issue 48, November 27, 1995.

15. Chiu, *op. cit.*

16. Weiss, *op. cit.*

17. Diana J. P. McKenzie, "Commerce On the Internet: Surfing Through Cyberspace Without Getting Wet," A review article by Gordon and Glickson P.C., Chicago, IL, 1995.

18. M. Fites, P. Kratz, and A. Brebner, "Control and Security of Computer Information Systems," Computer Science Press, 1989, referenced in *Site Security Handbook*. Site Security Policy Handbook Working Group RFC 1244, July 1991.

19. Marcus J. Ranum, "Internet Firewalls Frequently Asked Questions," http://www.iwi.com/pubs/faq.html.

Appendix C   Joint Ventures: Planning and Actions

1. E. A. (Ward) Sellers, *Structures for the Alliance: Corporate Commercial Considerations*, Federated Press Books and Conference Reports, Toronto, Ontario, Canada, April 1998.

2. A. Neil Campbell, *Governance, Exit and Regulatory Considerations*, Federated Press Books and Conference Reports, Toronto, Ontario, Canada, April 1998.

3. Richard E. Clark and Elliott Stikeman, *International Joint Ventures*, Federated Press Books and Conference Reports, Toronto, Ontario, Canada, April 1998.

4. Walter Blackwell, *Special Considerations in a Complex Technology Joint Venture*, Federated Press Books and Conference Reports, Toronto, Ontario, Canada, April 1998.

5. Joel Bleeke and David Ernst, *Collaborating to Compete: Using Strategic Alliances and Acquisitions in the Global Marketplace*, John Wiley & Sons Inc., New York, 1993.

6. James W. Botkin and Jana B. Mathews, *Winning Combinations: The Coming Wave of Entrepreneurial Partnerships Between Large and Small Companies*, John Wiley & Sons Inc., New York, 1992.

7. Timothy M. Collins and Thomas L. Doorley, *Teaming Up for the 90s: A Guide to International Joint Ventures and Strategic Alliances*, One Irwin, Homewood Business, Illinois, 1991.

8. Richard P. Cosma and John E. McDermott, *International Joint Ventures: The Legal and Tax Issues*, The Eurostudy Publishing Company, London, 1991.

9. P. W. Beamish, "The Characteristics of Joint Ventures in Developed and Developing Countries," *Columbia Journal of World Business*, 20: 13–19, 1985.

10. Donald W. Hendon and Rebecca Angeles Henden, *World Class Negotiating: Deal Making in the Global Marketplace*, John Wiley & Sons, Inc., New York, 1990.

11. R. F. Bresser, "Matching Collective and Competitive Strategies," *Strategic Management Jounral*, 9: 375–385, 1988.

12. A. I. Murray and C. Siehl, *Joint Venture and Other Alliances: Creating a Successful Cooperative Linkage*, Financial Executives Research Foundation, Morristown, N.J., 1989.

13. J. M. Geringer and L. Herbert, "Control and Performance of International Joint Ventures," *Journal of International Business Studies*, 20:2: 41–62, 1989.

14. Robert Porter Lynch, *The Practical Guide to Joint Ventures and Corporate Alliances*, John Wiley & Sons Inc., New York, 1989.

15. Michael H. Baniak, "Licensing and Ownership Agreements for Joint Ventures, Independent Contractors and Employees," papers from the Intellectual Property Licensing Seminar presented by the University of Dayton School of Law, February 18, 1999.

16. David W. Smith, *Structures for Alliances: Tax Considerations*, Federated Press Books and Conference Reports, Toronto, Ontario, Canada, April 1998.

17. Frank R. Fischer, *Contributions, Valuation, Dilution and Financing*, Federated Press Books and Conference Reports, Toronto, Ontario, Canada, April 1998.

18. Michael H. Baniak, 1999, *op. cit.*

19. Michael H. Baniak, 1999, *op. cit.*

20. Frank R. Fischer, 1998, *op. cit.*

21. Michael H. Baniak, 1999, *op. cit.*

22. Richard E. Clark and Elliott Stikeman, 1998, *op. cit.*

23. J. M. Geringer and L. Herbert, 1989, *op. cit.*

24. A. Parkhe, "Partner Nationality and Structure-Performance Relationship in Strategic Alliance," *Organization Science*, 4:2 May 1993.

25. Richard E. Clark and Elliott Stikeman, 1998, *op. cit.*

26. Garth M. Girvan and McCarthy Tetrault, *Joint Venture Acquisition Vehicles and Joint Bidding Arrangements*, Federated Press Books and Conference Reports, Toronto, Ontario, Canada, April 1998.

27. K. Singh, "The Impact of Technological Complexity and Interfirm Cooperation on Business Survival," *Academy of Management Best Paper Proceedings*, 67–71, 1995.

28. E. A. (Ward) Sellers, 1998, *op. cit.*

29. A. Neil Campbell, 1998, *op. cit.*

30. J. Greenberg, "Organizational Justice: Yesterday, Today and Tomorrow," *Journal of Management*, 16: 399–432, 1990a.

31. B. Gomes-Casseres, "Joint Venture Instability: Is It a Problem?" *Columbia Journal of World Business*, Summer, 97–101.

32. Michael H. Baniak, 1999, *op. cit.*

Index

.